goodfood
eatwell

FAMILY FREEZER
MEALS

D1063638

BBC good food eat well

FAMILY FREEZER MEALS

BOOKS

10 9 8 7 6 5 4 3

BBC Books, an imprint of Ebury Publishing
20 Vauxhall Bridge Road,
London SW1V 2SA

BBC Books is part of the Penguin Random House
group of companies whose addresses can be
found at global.penguinrandomhouse.com

Penguin
Random House
UK

Photographs © BBC Magazines 2018
Recipes © BBC Worldwide 2018
Book design © Woodlands Books Ltd 2018
All recipes contained in this book first appeared in
BBC *Good Food* magazine.

First published by BBC Books in 2018

www.eburypublishing.co.uk

A CIP catalogue record for this book is available
from the British Library

ISBN 9781785943324

Origination by Born Group, London

Printed and bound in China by C&C Offset Printing
Co, Ltd.

Typeset in India by Integra Software Services Pvt.
Ltd, Pondicherry

Cover Design: Interstate Creative Partners Ltd
Production: Alex Merrett

Penguin Random House is committed to a
sustainable future for our business, our readers and
our planet. This book is made from Forest
Stewardship Council® certified paper.

BBC Books would like to thank the following people
for providing photos. While every effort has been
made to trace and acknowledge all photographers,
we should like to apologise should there be any
errors or omissions.

Will Heap 14, 28, 62, 64, 84, 86, 130, 134, 150, 152,
178, 180, 182, 184, 186, 284, 286; David Munns 16, 50,
70, 132, 140, 166, 188, 192, 254, 312; Tom Regester
18, 90, 98, 100, 102, 158, 238, 308; Mike English 22,
66, 72, 80, 88, 94, 104, 106, 108, 116, 120, 122, 124,
142, 156, 234, 236, 260, 276; Stuart Ovenden 24,
44, 46, 60, 112, 114,148, 196, 240, 264, 292, 304;
Darren Feist 26; Sam Stowell 30, 32, 34, 36, 38, 42,
52, 160, 162, 242, 310; Rob Streeter 54,126, 128, 144,
146, 262; Philip Webb 56; Maja Smend 68, 82, 154;
Lis Parsons 78, 136, 282, 252; Myles New 92, 290;
Peter Cassidy 96, 138, 200, 246, 296, 300; Toby Scott
110; Gareth Morgans 168; Phillip Webb 174; Charlie
Richards 176; Gareth Morgans 190; Yuki Sugiura 248;
Howard Shooter 256; Adrien Lawrence 258; Clare
Winfield 302.

All the recipes in this book were created by the
editorial team at Good Food and by regular
contributors to BBC Magazines.

Contents

Introduction

· ·

The freezer is perhaps the most useful, yet underrated, piece of kitchen equipment that exists. At BBC *Good Food*, we know how much our readers appreciate being able to get ahead and prepare in advance, which is one reason why we always highlight dishes that freeze particularly well and give tips where appropriate in our magazine and on our website, to help you make the most of our recipes. This book pulls together all of our very best freezable meals, sides and puddings into one handy edition.

For those of us with busy lives, a well-stocked freezer is a welcome help on hectic weeknights. Pulling out a delicious homemade dinner is much quicker than the time it would take to phone for a takeaway – not to mention that it's often far cheaper.

But freezer food is not just for quick, budget-friendly weeknight dinners – we've included recipes for every occasion, including breakfasts and brunches, crowd pleasers, soups and lighter bites, vegetarian and vegan dishes and dinner-party worthy desserts.

All of our recipes are triple-tested in our very own test kitchen to ensure that they work every time for you. We've also included a full nutritional breakdown for each one, so you can keep track of the calorie, fat and salt content.

With so many delicious dishes at your fingertips, what are you waiting for? Roll up those sleeves, get cooking and stock up that freezer!

Notes & conversions

NOTES ON THE RECIPES
- Eggs are large in the UK and Australia and extra large in America unless stated.
- Wash fresh produce before preparation.
- Recipes contain nutritional analyses for 'sugars', which means the total sugar content including all natural sugars in the ingredients, unless otherwise stated.

APPROXIMATE LIQUID CONVERSION

Metric	Imperial	Aus	US
50ml	2 fl oz	¼ cup	¼ cup
125ml	4 fl oz	½ cup	½ cup
175ml	6 fl oz	¾ cup	¾ cup
225ml	8 fl oz	1 cup	1 cup
300ml	10 fl oz/½ pint	½ pint	1¼ cups
450ml	16 fl oz	2 cups	2 cups/1 pint
600ml	20 fl oz/1 pint	1 pint	2½ cups
1 litre	35 fl oz/1¾ pints	1¾ pints	1 quart

OVEN TEMPERATURE CONVERSION

GAS	°C	°C FAN	°F	OVEN TEMP.
¼	110	90	225	Very cool
½	120	100	250	Very cool
1	140	120	275	Cool or slow
2	150	130	300	Cool or slow
3	160	140	325	Warm
4	180	160	350	Moderate
5	190	170	375	Moderately hot
6	200	180	400	Fairly hot
7	220	200	425	Hot
8	230	210	450	Very hot
9	240	220	475	Very hot

APPROXIMATE WEIGHT CONVERSIONS
Cup measurements, which are used in Australia and America, have not been listed here as they vary from ingredient to ingredient. Kitchen scales should be used to measure dry/solid ingredients.

SPOON MEASURES
Spoon measurements are level unless otherwise specifed.
- 1 teaspoon (tsp) = 5ml
- 1 tablespoon (tbsp) = 15ml
- 1 Australian tablespoon = 20ml (cooks in Australia should measure 3 teaspoons where 1 tablespoon is specifed in a recipe)

Good Food is concerned about sustainable sourcing and animal welfare. Where possible, humanely reared meats, sustainably caught fish (see fishonline.org for further information from the Marine Conservation Society) and free- range chickens and eggs are used when recipes are originally tested.

Advice on freezing & reheating

HOW TO FREEZE
Make the most of your freezer by freezing things properly following our handy hints and tips.

TOP FREEZING TIPS
Whether you have a chest or upright freezer or just a tiny icebox at the top of the fridge, the principles of successful freezing are the same.

1 Cool foods properly before you freeze them. Freezing hot or warm food will only increase the temperature of the freezer and could cause other foods around them to start defrosting.

2 Only refreeze food if you will cook it thoroughly in between freezes, for example if you defrost mince to make Bolognese and then freeze the finished dish you will have cooked the mince thoroughly.

3 A full freezer is more economical to run as the cold air doesn't need to circulate so much, so less power is needed. If you have lots of space free, fill the freezer with everyday items you're bound to use, such as sliced bread or frozen peas and other veg.

4 Make sure you wrap foods properly or put them in sealed containers, otherwise your food can get freezer-burn. Food should be wrapped tightly in cling film, if you use freezer bags then squash out any air before sealing them and choose containers that fit their contents with only a little room for expansion.

5 Freeze food in realistically sized portions. You don't want to have to defrost a stew big enough to feed eight when you're only feeding a family of three. If in doubt freeze single portions, you can always defrost more than one at once.

6 Err on the side of caution if you find an unnamed bag of something in the freezer. Contrary to what many people think, freezing doesn't kill bacteria. If you are unsure of how long something has been frozen or are a bit wary of something once defrosted, don't take any chances.

7 Freezing won't improve the quality of your food so don't freeze old food because you don't want to waste it; the point of freezing is to keep food at its prime. If you have leftovers then freeze them straight away.

DEFROSTING
An icy freezer is an inefficient one, so make sure you defrost your freezer if ice builds up. Don't worry about the food; most things will remain frozen in the fridge for a couple of hours while the freezer defrosts.

LABELS
It may seem a bother at the time, but unless you label you might not remember what it is, let alone when it was frozen. Buy a blue marker for raw foods and a red marker for cooked foods. You don't have to write an essay, just label the food clearly. You can use big-lettered abbreviations, for example a big red P means cooked pork or a blue F means raw fish. And always add the date it was frozen.

POWER CUTS
The manufacturer's handbook will tell you what the holding time is for your freezer so check it. If there has been a power cut or you think the freezer has been turned off at some point, don't open the door. Generally foods should remain frozen in the freezer for about 24 hours, leaving you time to get to the bottom of the problem.

WHAT NOT TO FREEZE
Most individual ingredients can be frozen, however, some foods simply aren't freezer friendly:

Raw eggs in their shells will expand and crack.

Hard-boiled eggs go rubbery. If they are within recipes you may like to remove them before freezing and cook new ones when you reheat your dish.

Vegetables with a high water content, such as lettuce, cucumber, bean sprouts and radishes, go limp and mushy.

Soft herbs, like parsley, basil and chives, are fine for incorporating in dishes but won't be good for garnishes. Stir any garnishes on leftovers through the dish before freezing.

GREAT TO FREEZE
Butter and margarine can be frozen for 3 months.

Grated cheese can be frozen for up to 4 months and can be used straight from the freezer.

Most bread will freeze well for up to 3 months. Sliced bread can be toasted from frozen.

Milk will freeze for 1 month. Defrost in the fridge and shake well before using.

Raw pastry will freeze for up to 6 months and takes just 1 hour to thaw.

COOKING FROM FROZEN
Freezer management is all about forward planning, but some dishes can be cooked straight from frozen. When cooking food from frozen, use a lower temperature to start with to thaw, then increase the temperature to cook. Foods include:

Soups, stews, braises and casseroles.
Bakes, gratins and potato-topped pies.

FOODS THAT SHOULD NEVER BE COOKED FROM FROZEN
Raw poultry, large joints of meat.

REHEATING
When it comes to eating up your leftovers, how you handle them is key to staying healthy.

If you're taking leftovers from the freezer, eat within 24 hours. Make sure they're thoroughly defrosted before heating, by leaving them in the fridge or using a microwave.

Reheat food until piping hot throughout. If you're using a microwave, be aware they do not heat evenly throughout, so take your food out halfway through the cooking time and give it a stir. Foods should be heated until they reach and maintain 70C or above for 2 minutes.

Hash browns

Crispy hash browns are a must for the full English breakfast. With just three ingredients and being freezeable, too, they're easy to add to your next fry up.

EASY ⏱ PREP 10 mins COOK 20 mins plus cooling ◷ MAKES 8 (SERVES 4)

- 3 medium-sized potatoes (approx. 370g in total, unpeeled, left whole – Maris Pipers, King Edward and Desirée are all good choices)
- 50g butter, melted
- 4 tbsp sunflower oil

1 Cook the potatoes in a saucepan of boiling water for 10 mins, then drain and set aside until they are cool enough to handle.
2 Coarsely grate the potatoes into a bowl discarding any skin that comes off in your hand as you grate. Season well with salt and pepper and pour over half the butter. Mix well then divide the mix into 8 and shape into patties or squares. The hash browns can be prepared a day ahead and chilled until ready to cook or frozen for up to a month. Freeze flat on trays then transfer to freezer bags.
3 To cook, heat the oil and the remaining butter in a frying pan until sizzling and gently fry the hash browns, in batches if needed, for 4–5 mins on each side until crisp and golden. Serve straight away or leave in a low oven to keep warm.

Nutrition per serving
kcal 264 • fat 21g • saturates 8g • carbs 16g • sugars 1g • fibre 2g • protein 2g • salt 0.4g

Teacakes

. . . .

Teacakes don't have to be eaten at teatime, toast them with butter for breakfast.

MORE EFFORT ⏱ PREP 10 mins plus resting COOK 25 mins ⏲ MAKES 6

- 100ml milk
- 30g butter
- 350g strong white bread flour
- 7g sachet fast-action dried yeast
- 2 tbsp sugar
- ½ tsp mixed spice
- 75g mixed dried fruit (peel, sultanas, raisins and currants)
- oil, for greasing
- 1 egg, beaten

1 Warm the milk with the butter in a pan until the butter has melted, then add 100ml water to cool the mixture to room temp. Tip the flour, yeast, sugar, spice and 1 tsp salt into a bowl, making sure the yeast is on the other side of the bowl to the salt. Make a well in the flour mixture and pour the milk and butter in, mixing until it forms big flakes, then bring together with your hands. Tip on a surface and knead until smooth (about 5 mins). Put the dough into a large, lightly oiled bowl, cover with a damp tea towel and leave until doubled in size, so about 1–1½ hours.

2 Line a tray with baking paper. Tip the mixed dried fruits into the dough and knead them in, trying to disperse them evenly throughout the dough. Cut your dough into 6 even-sized balls, take each ball and, using the cup of your hand, and pressing down a little with your palm, roll the ball in a circular motion on the surface to create tension across the top of the bun and a neat round shape. Place onto a tray about 5cm away from each other and press down with your palm to flatten the dough down a little, creating the teacake shape. Cover loosely with an oiled sheet of cling film, for a further 45 mins, or until they have doubled in size.

3 Meanwhile, heat the oven to 200C/180C fan/gas 6. Brush the top of each bun liberally with the egg wash, then bake for 20 mins on the top shelf of the oven, until the buns are golden and well risen. Allow to cool on a wire rack, then slice in half, toast and slather with butter if you like. These can be frozen once cooked, half them first and you can put them under the grill frozen.

. . . .

Nutrition per teacake
kcal 338 • fat 6g • saturates 3g • carbs 60g • sugars 16g • fibre 2g • protein 10g • salt 1g

Vegan breakfast muffins

These easy vegan breakfast muffins with muesli and pecans are perfect for making ahead of time and freezing in batches for a quick morning snack.

EASY ⏱ PREP 25 mins COOK 25 mins ⬛ MAKES 12

- 150g muesli mix
- 50g light brown soft sugar
- 160g plain flour
- 1 tsp baking powder
- 250ml sweetened soy milk
- 1 apple, peeled and grated
- 2 tbsp grapeseed oil
- 3 tbsp nut butter (we used almond)
- 4 tbsp demerara sugar
- 50g pecans, roughly chopped

1 Heat the oven to 200C/180C fan/gas 6. Line a muffin tin with cases. Mix 100g muesli with the light brown sugar, flour and baking powder in a bowl. Combine the milk, apple, oil and 2 tbsp nut butter in a jug, then stir into the dry mixture. Divide equally among the cases. Mix the remaining muesli with the demerara sugar, remaining nut butter and the pecans, and spoon over the muffins.

2 Bake for 25–30 mins or until the muffins are risen and golden. *Will keep for 2 to 3 days in an airtight container or freeze for 1 month. Refresh in the oven before serving.*

Nutrition per muffin
kcal 224 • fat 9g • saturates 1g • carbs 30g • sugars 15g • fibre 2g • protein 4g • salt 0.1g

Rustic oat & treacle soda bread

This simple, yeast-free Irish bread is delicious with butter and jam. For a darker loaf, you can use an extra spoonful of treacle in place of the honey.

EASY ⏲ PREP 10 mins COOK 30 mins 🕒 CUTS INTO 12 SLICES

- oil or butter, for greasing
- 250g plain flour, plus extra for dusting
- 200g wholemeal flour
- 50g porridge oats, plus extra for sprinkling
- 1 tsp bicarbonate of soda
- 150ml pot live bio yogurt
- 1 tbsp black treacle
- 1 tbsp clear honey

1 Heat oven to 200C/180C fan/gas 6 and grease a baking sheet. Put the flours, oats, bicarb and 1 tsp salt in a large bowl and stir to combine. Tip the yogurt into a jug, add enough water to make it up to 400ml and mix well. Stir the treacle and honey into the yogurt mixture until they dissolve. Pour onto the dry ingredients and stir with a round-bladed knife until you have a soft, sticky dough.

2 Tip onto a lightly floured surface and lightly form the dough into a round. Lift onto the baking sheet, cut a deep cross in the dough and sprinkle with oats. Bake for 30 mins or until the crust is golden and the loaf sounds hollow when tapped underneath. Soda bread should be eaten the same day, or toasted the next. Alternatively freeze single slices to toast as you need them.

Nutrition per slice
kcal 173 • fat 2g • saturates 1g • carbs 33g • sugars 4g • fibre 3g • protein 6g • salt 0.7g

Cardamom buns

This spiced Swedish bun has an intense floral perfume from cardamom seeds, which works its way into the dough during cooking.

MORE EFFORT ⏱ PREP 40 mins plus at least 2 hrs proving and rising COOK 25 mins ◳ MAKES 12

- 35 cardamom pods
- 350ml full-fat milk
- 200g butter, cubed, at room temperature
- 500g strong white bread flour, plus extra for dusting
- 225g golden caster sugar
- 7g sachet fast-action dried yeast
- ½ tsp ground cinnamon
- vegetable oil or sunflower oil, for greasing
- 1 large egg, beaten
- 2 tbsp pearl sugar (can be bought from the baking aisle, use crushed sugar lumps instead if you like)

1 Crack 10 cardamom pods with a pestle and mortar, and tip into a pan. Add the milk and warm until steaming. Add 50g butter and set aside, swirling the pan to melt the butter.

2 Put the flour, 75g of the sugar, the yeast, cinnamon and ½ tsp salt into a bowl or freestanding mixer and mix. When the milk is cool, strain into the flour, discarding the cardamom. Using a wooden spoon or dough hook, mix to form a soft dough. Tip out and knead for 10 mins, or run the mixer for 5 mins, until smooth and stretchy. Clean the bowl, grease, then return the dough to the bowl and turn over until coated. Cover with a tea towel to rise for 2 hrs or until doubled (you can prove in the fridge overnight).

3 Crack the remaining cardamom pods and tip just the seeds into the mortar. Crush to a powder, then combine with 150g sugar. Mix the butter with all but 2 tbsp of this sugar.

4 Line 2 baking trays with parchment. Punch the dough to knock out the air and roll to a 35 x 45cm rectangle, with the longer edge facing you. Spread the cardamom butter over, right to the edges. Fold the top third down to the middle and the bottom third up, like an envelope, so you have 3 layers of dough. Score, then cut into 12 strips, 3.5 x 11cm each. Cut each strip down the centre, leaving it attached at the top. Twist each strip away from the centre 2 or 3 times, then tie the dough in a knot and tuck the ends underneath the bun. Put on the tray when done.

5 Cover trays with oiled cling film and rise in a warm place for 1 hr until doubled. Heat oven to 190C/170C fan/gas 5.

6 Uncover the buns and brush all over with the egg, then sprinkle with pearl sugar. Bake for 20–25 mins until golden – swap the trays halfway through if browning unevenly.

7 Bring the cardamom sugar and 50ml water to the boil, then remove from the heat, swirling to dissolve the sugar. Brush over the buns 2 or 3 times as they cool, then leave to soak for 20 mins before eating. Keep for 2 days in a container or freeze for 2 months. Defrost at room temp and reheat for 5 mins in the oven.

Nutrition per bun
kcal 381 • fat 16g • saturates 10g • carbs 52g • sugars 20g • fibre 1g • protein 7g • salt 0.6g

Plain waffles

Easy homemade waffles to serve with fruit, syrup and sauces to your heart's content.

EASY ⊙ PREP 15 mins COOK 30 mins ⊙ MAKES ABOUT 10 WAFFLES

- 4 large eggs, separated
- 300g plain flour
- ½ tsp bicarbonate of soda
- 2 tbsp golden caster sugar
- 50g butter, melted
- 600ml semi-skimmed milk

1 Heat the waffle maker according to manufacturer's instructions. Whisk the egg whites to stiff peaks. In a separate large bowl, mix together the flour, bicarbonate, caster sugar and a pinch of salt. Make a well in the centre and add the egg yolks and melted butter. Start mixing with a balloon whisk; keep whisking as you slowly add the milk until you get a smooth, thick batter. Carefully fold in the egg whites with a metal spoon.

2 Heat oven to 180C/160C fan/gas 4. Use a ladle to pour the batter into your waffle maker and cook for 5 mins or according to the manufacturer's instructions. Repeat until all the batter has been used up, placing your finished waffles onto a baking tray as you go. If you want to freeze your waffles cool them and wrap them tightly in cling film first.

3 Once all the waffles are made, transfer to the oven for 5 mins to warm through and crisp. Serve with sweet or savoury toppings.

Nutrition per waffle
kcal 218 • fat 7g • saturates 4g • carbs 30g • sugars 7g • fibre 1g • protein 8g • salt 0.4g

Seeded wholemeal soda bread

Shop-bought bread can be loaded with salt, sugar and preservatives, so try making your own for a healthier loaf. It takes only 10 minutes to prepare.

EASY ⏲ PREP 10 mins COOK 25 mins ⏲ CUTS INTO 10 SLICES

- 450g wholemeal flour, plus extra for dusting
- 75g four-seed mix (sesame, sunflower, golden linseed and pumpkin)
- 1 tsp bicarbonate of soda
- 1 tbsp black treacle
- 150ml pot natural bio yogurt, made up to 450ml with water

1 Heat oven to 200C/180C fan/gas 6 and line a baking sheet with baking parchment. Put the flour, seeds, bicarbonate of soda and a pinch of salt in a large bowl and mix to combine. Stir the treacle into the yogurt mixture and, when the treacle dissolves, pour onto the dry ingredients. Stir together with the blade of a knife until you have a soft, sticky dough. Leave for 5 mins (this allows time for the liquid to absorb into the bran).

2 Tip onto a lightly floured surface and form the dough into a round about 18cm across. It will still be very sticky, so don't over-handle it – treat it like scone dough rather than bread dough. Lift onto the baking sheet and bake for 25–30 mins until the crust is golden and the loaf sounds hollow when tapped underneath. Freeze any leftover bread cut into individual slices.

Nutrition per slice
kcal 183 • fat 4g • saturates 1g • carbs 27g • sugars 3g • fibre 5g • protein 7g • salt 0.3g

Blueberry Bakewell muffins

These easy blueberry muffins have a delightfully jammy centre and crunchy crumble topping.

EASY ⏱ PREP 20 mins COOK 20 mins plus cooling ◔ MAKES 12

- 100g unsalted butter, softened, plus 1 tbsp, melted, for greasing
- 140g golden caster sugar
- 2 large eggs
- 140g natural yogurt
- 1 tsp vanilla extract
- 1 tsp almond extract
- 2 tbsp milk
- 250g plain flour
- 2 tsp baking powder
- 1 tsp bicarbonate of soda
- 125g pack blueberries (or use frozen)

FOR THE TOPPING
- 3 tbsp demerara sugar
- ¼ tsp ground cinnamon
- 3 tbsp flaked almonds, roughly chopped
- 2 tbsp ground almonds
- 3 tbsp plain flour
- 1 tbsp cold butter, diced
- 12 tsp wild blueberry conserve

1 Heat oven to 200C/180C fan/gas 6 and line a 12-hole muffin tin with paper cases. Put all the topping ingredients, apart from the jam, in a bowl and rub together.

2 Beat the butter and caster sugar together until pale and fluffy. Add the eggs and beat in for 1 min, then mix in the yogurt, extracts and milk. Combine the flour, baking powder and bicarb in a bowl with ¼ tsp fine salt, then tip this into the wet ingredients and stir in. Finally, fold in the blueberries and divide the mixture among the muffin cases. Top each muffin with 1 tsp blueberry jam, then scatter over the crumble mixture.

3 Bake for 5 mins, then reduce oven to 180C/160C fan/gas 4 and bake for 15–18 mins more until risen and golden, and a cocktail stick inserted in comes out with just jam on it – no wet cake mixture.

4 Cool in the tin for 10 mins, then carefully lift out onto a wire rack to finish cooling. Will keep for 3–4 days in an airtight container. To freeze, cool completely and then seal in freezer bags; refresh in a hot oven.

Nutrition per muffin
kcal 312 • fat 14g • saturates 6g • carbs 40g • sugars 24g • fibre 1g • protein 6g • salt 0.6g

Sourdough bread

Making a sourdough starter from scratch couldn't be simpler with our step-by-step recipe for a chewy, flavoursome loaf.

A CHALLENGE 🕐 PREP 1 hr plus 8 days for the starter and 9 hrs rising COOK 40 mins 🕒 CUTS INTO 12 SLICES

FOR THE STARTER
• 700g strong white flour

FOR THE LOAF
• 500g strong white flour, plus extra for dusting
• 1 tsp fine salt
• 1 tbsp clear honey
• 300g sourdough starter
• flavourless oil, for greasing

1 Whisk 100g of flour with 125ml slightly warm water until smooth and lump-free. Transfer the starter to a 1-litre jar or plastic container. Leave the lid ajar for 1 hr in a warm place (around 25C is ideal), seal and leave for 24 hrs.

2 For the next 6 days, 'feed' the starter. Each day, tip away half the starter, add an extra 100g flour and 125ml slightly warm water and stir. Try to do at the same time every day.

3 After 3–4 days you should see bubbles and smell yeast and a little acidity. This indicates the starter is working! On day 7, it should be bubbly and smell sweeter. It is now ready.

4 Tip the flour, 225ml warm water, the salt, honey and starter into a bowl or a mixer with a dough hook. Stir with a wooden spoon or slowly in the machine until combined – add extra flour if too sticky or extra warm water if too dry.

5 Tip onto a lightly floured surface and knead for 10 mins until soft and elastic – you should be able to stretch it without tearing. If using a mixer, turn up and mix for 5 mins.

6 Place in an oiled bowl, covered with oiled cling film. Leave in a warm place for 3 hrs. You may not see much action, but don't worry, sourdough takes a long time to rise.

7 Line a bowl with a clean tea towel and flour really well or, if you have a proving basket, use this. Tip the dough back onto your work surface and knead briefly to knock out any air. Shape into a smooth ball and dust with flour.

8 Place the dough, seam-side up, in the bowl or proving basket, cover with a sheet of oiled cling film and leave at room temperature for 6–8 hrs until roughly doubled in size.

9 Place a baking tray in the oven and heat to 230C/210C fan/gas 8. Fill a roasting tin with water and place in the bottom of the oven to create steam. Remove the tray from the oven, sprinkle with flour, then tip the dough on the tray.

10 Slash the top a few times with a knife, then bake for about 35–40 mins until golden. It will sound hollow when tapped on the bottom. Leave to cool on a wire rack for 20 mins. Freeze the bread whole or in individual slices.

Nutrition per slice
kcal 245 • fat 1g • saturates 0g • carbs 48g • sugars 1g • fibre 2g • protein 8g • salt 0.4g

Cheese & Marmite scones

Marmite gives a deep savoury flavour to these tasty pinwheel cheddar cheese scones – try them warm spread with cold butter.

EASY 🕐 PREP 20 mins plus cooling COOK 12 mins 🕐 MAKES 8

- 450g plain flour, plus extra for dusting
- 1 tbsp baking powder
- 3 tsp Marmite
- 1 large egg
- about 250ml milk
- 1 tbsp sunflower oil
- 140g mature cheddar, grated
- 100g full-fat cream cheese

1 Heat oven to 220C/200C fan/gas 7 and dust a baking tray with a little flour. Mix the flour and baking powder in a large bowl. Put 1 tsp Marmite in a jug, add the egg and make up to 300ml with the milk. Stir in the oil, then beat really well to dissolve the Marmite.

2 Tip 85g of the cheddar into a bowl and mix with the cream cheese and remaining Marmite to make a spread. Toss the rest of the cheese through the flour mixture, then pour in the milk mixture and stir with the blade of a knife until it comes together. (You need to work quickly once you've added the liquid, as it activates the baking powder.) Tip onto a lightly floured work surface and gently knead the mix, taking care not to overwork it, as it will make the scones heavy.

3 Press or lightly roll the dough into an oblong about 20 x 25cm. Spread with the Marmite mixture and roll up from the longest side to create a tight, fat cylinder. Pat the ends of the cylinder to straighten them, then slice into 8 pinwheels and put on the baking tray, patting them to make flattish rounds. Bake for 12–15 mins until golden and cooked.

4 Leave for a few mins on the tray to allow the cheese centre to harden a little, then transfer to a wire rack to cool. Eat warm or cold. Best eaten on the day they are made or frozen and refreshed in a hot oven.

Nutrition per scone
kcal 370 • fat 15g • saturates 8g • carbs 44g • sugars 2g • fibre 2g • protein 13g • salt 1.1g

Almond & raspberry cruffins

Cross a croissant with a muffin and you'll get these buttery, flaky, fruity pastries – perfect for brunch or an indulgent treat.

MORE EFFORT ⏱ PREP 40 mins plus chilling COOK 20 mins 🕒 MAKES 6

FOR THE PASTRY
- 1 tsp fast-action dried yeast
- 1 tsp lemon juice
- 225g strong white flour, sifted, plus extra for shaping
- 25g golden caster sugar
- 140g cold unsalted butter, chopped into sugar-cube-sized pieces

FOR THE FILLING (OPTIONAL BUT WORTH IT!)
- 50g unsalted butter
- 50g golden caster sugar
- 50g ground almonds
- 1 tsp plain flour
- a few drops almond extract
- 1 egg yolk

TO SERVE
- a few tbsp seedless raspberry jam
- icing sugar, to dust

1 Measure 75ml just-warm water, add the yeast and stir to dissolve. Measure another 75ml ice-cold water and add the lemon juice. Mix the flour and sugar with ½ tsp fine salt in a bowl, then toss in the butter until coated in the flour. Splash the yeast and lemon waters into the bowl. Using a round-bladed knife, work quickly to bring the mix to a rough dough with lumps of butter held inside it. Turn onto a floured work surface, shape into a squat rectangle (don't knead too much), then wrap in cling film and freeze for 15 mins.

2 Dust the work surface and pastry with flour. Roll the pastry in one direction until it's 3 times as long as it is wide, or about 45 x 15cm. Try to keep the sides straight as you roll, and the top and bottom edges as square as possible.

3 Fold the pastry over itself. Fold the bottom third up, then the top third down, to make a block. Turn so that its open edge is facing right, like a book. Press the edges together with the rolling pin. Roll out and fold the pastry like this 3 more times to make a smooth dough, with the odd streak of butter. If it feels greasy or springy at any point, cover and chill for 10 mins before continuing. Wrap and chill for at least 1 hr.

4 Beat the filling ingredients with a pinch of salt. Put the dough on a floured work surface. Cut in half across the middle and return one half to the fridge. Roll the other to a 30 x 20cm rectangle, then cut into 3 strips, 10cm wide. To create more layers, fold each piece in half lengthways. Put a generous tsp of the filling at one end, then roll the pastry around it in a spiral. Place, cut-edge up, into a non-stick muffin tin. Repeat to make 6 cruffins. Cover with cling film. Can be chilled overnight (leftover filling can be frozen.)

5 Prove the dough at a cool room temperature for 2 hrs or until the pastry has filled the wells of the tin. Heat oven to 190C/170C fan/gas 5. Bake for 20–25 mins until risen and deep golden. Remove and cool a little on a rack. Spoon the jam into a piping bag with a 5mm nozzle. Push the nozzle into the middle of the cruffin and squeeze. Dust with icing sugar and eat on the day of baking. Freeze leftovers in bags and refresh in a hot oven once defrosted.

Nutrition per cruffin
kcal 501 • fat 32g • saturates 17g • carbs 45g • sugars 18g • fibre 1g • protein 8g • salt 0.5g

Seeded wholemeal loaf

This hearty, wholesome bread is rich in flavour and packed with seeds – try pumpkin, sunflower, poppy or linseeds.

MORE EFFORT ⏱ PREP 35 mins COOK 45 mins plus cooling and 1 hr 45 mins rising ◷ CUTS INTO 10-12 SLICES

- 400g strong wholemeal bread flour
- 100g spelt flour
- 7g sachet fast-action dried yeast
- 1 tbsp black treacle
- oil, for greasing
- 50g mixed seeds (we used pumpkin, sunflower, poppy and linseeds)
- 1 egg yolk, loosened with a fork

1 Combine both flours in a large bowl with the yeast and 1 tsp fine salt. Mix the treacle with 250ml warm water until well combined. Stir into the flour to make a slightly sticky dough. If you need to add more water, splash it in 1 tbsp at a time.

2 Knead the dough on a lightly floured surface for 10 mins (or in a tabletop mixer for 5–7 mins). Your dough should be smooth and elastic when it's ready. Place the dough in a lightly oiled bowl, flip the dough over to coat it in oil, then cover with a sheet of oiled cling film. Leave in a warm place until doubled in size – this will take about 1 hr. Lightly oil a 900g loaf tin.

3 Once doubled in size, knead the dough again for 3–5 mins to knock out the air bubbles – add most of the seeds and work these into the dough as you knead. Shape the dough into an oval roughly the same length as your tin. Place in the tin and leave to prove, covered with oiled cling film, for 30–45 mins until it has nearly doubled in size again. Heat oven to 200C/180C fan/gas 6.

4 Gently press a finger into the loaf to check if it has had enough proving time. When it's ready, glaze the top of the loaf with the egg yolk and sprinkle over the remaining seeds. Bake in the oven for 40–45 mins until golden brown – if you tip the loaf out of the tin and tap the bottom, it should sound hollow. Leave to cool on a wire rack for at least 30 mins before slicing. This loaf will freeze whole or can be sliced.

Nutrition per slice (12)
kcal 173 • fat 3g • saturates 1g • carbs 27g • sugars 2g • fibre 5g • protein 7g • salt 0.4g

Cheat's sourdough

Don't be daunted by making a sourdough bread starter at home – this easy, overnight version makes a lovely loaf.

MORE EFFORT ⏱ PREP 30 mins plus overnight fermenting and rising COOK 25 mins ⟳ CUTS INTO 10-12 SLICES

FOR THE STARTER
- 100g strong white bread flour
- 100g organic dark rye flour
- ½ x 7g sachet fast-action dried yeast

FOR THE MAIN DOUGH
- 400g strong white bread flour
- ½ x 7g sachet fast-action dried yeast

1 To make your starter, place all the ingredients in a bowl and add 250ml cold water. Mix together thoroughly with a spoon until you have a spongy mixture, then cover with cling film and leave at room temperature at least overnight, but up to 24 hrs if you have time.

2 To make the bread dough, tip the ingredients into a clean bowl and add 1 tbsp fine salt, 200ml cold water and your starter. Bring all the ingredients together to a dough, adding a splash more water if too stiff, then tip out onto a lightly floured surface and knead for at least 10 mins until smooth, elastic and springy (this will take 5–7 mins in a mixer with a dough hook). Place the dough in a clean, lightly oiled bowl, cover with cling film and leave until doubled in size – about 1 hr at room temperature, 3 hrs in the fridge.

3 Tip the dough onto a floured surface and gently shape into a round – you don't want to knock too much air out of the dough. Dust a piece of baking parchment heavily with flour and sit the dough on top. Cover with a tea towel and leave to prove for 1 hr until doubled in size.

4 Heat oven to 220C/200C fan/gas 7. Place a sturdy flat baking tray on the middle shelf of the oven and a smaller tray with sides underneath. Dust the dough with flour and slash with a utility knife. Slide the bread onto the hot tray on top and throw a few ice cubes (or pour some cold water) onto the tray below – this creates a burst of steam, which helps the bread form a nice crust. Bake for 25–30 mins until the loaf sounds hollow when tapped on the bottom. Leave the bread to cool completely. Will freeze as a loaf or cut into slices.

Nutrition per slice (12)
kcal 172 • fat 1g • saturates 0g • carbs 33g • sugars 0g • fibre 3g • protein 6g • salt 1.3g

Gluten-free chilli cornbread

Golden polenta and frozen sweetcorn make a deliciously different alternative to your regular loaf – best eaten fresh from the oven.

MORE EFFORT ⏱ PREP 20 mins plus at least 2 hrs soaking COOK 30 mins ⏲ SERVES 4-6

- 200g polenta or fine ground cornmeal
- 284ml pot buttermilk
- 25g butter
- 1 red chilli, deseeded and finely chopped
- 1 tsp baking powder (look for a gluten-free one)
- ¼ tsp bicarbonate of soda
- 50g frozen sweetcorn, defrosted
- 2 large eggs, beaten

1 Lightly toast the polenta in a dry frying pan for 3–4 mins, stirring to ensure even cooking, until the polenta has heated through, is fragrant and small patches are starting to turn golden brown. Take off the heat, tip half into a large bowl and add the buttermilk. Stir well, cover and leave to soak for 2–3 hrs.

2 Melt the butter in a 25cm ovenproof frying pan (a cast-iron one is perfect) and heat oven to 220C/200C fan/gas 7. Stir the butter and the remaining ingredients, including the rest of the toasted polenta and ½ tsp salt, into the buttermilk and polenta mixture. (Don't wipe out the frying pan – the slick of butter will ensure the bread doesn't stick.)

3 Put the pan back on the heat and turn up the temperature. Pour the mixture into the pan – it should sizzle as it hits it, like a Yorkshire pudding. Put the whole pan in the oven and bake for 15–20 mins until golden brown and firm in the middle. Leave to cool a little, then serve cut into wedges. To freeze, cool completely and then wrap in cling film. Reheat to serve.

Nutrition per serving (6)
kcal 200 • fat 6g • saturates 3g • carbs 29g • sugars 3g • fibre 1g • protein 7g • salt 1g

No-knead beginner's loaf

This easy Italian-inspired bread is designed to fit into the working week. Leave out the rosemary if you prefer.

EASY ⏱ PREP 10 mins plus cooling and at least 9 hrs rising COOK 1 hr ⏰ CUTS INTO 10-12 SLICES

- ¼ tsp fast-action dried yeast
- 500g strong white bread flour, plus extra for dusting
- 3–4 rosemary sprigs, leaves picked (optional)
- 2 tsp sea salt
- 2 tbsp olive oil

1 Pour 500ml warm water into a large bowl and sprinkle over the yeast. Stir to distribute the yeast, then add the flour, rosemary leaves and sea salt. Once everything is well mixed, cover the bowl with cling film and leave to rise overnight, or for 8–12 hrs.

2 Once the dough has risen, brush the inside of another large bowl with the olive oil and dust with 1–2 tbsp flour. Carefully tip the bread into the floured bowl and dust the top with more flour. Cover again with cling film and leave to prove for 1 hr.

3 Heat oven to 200C/180C fan/gas 6. Place a large casserole dish, small roasting tin or cake tin in the oven to heat up. When it's really hot, take it out of the oven and quickly tip in the dough. (The dish or tin should be hot enough that the dough will sizzle when it goes in.)

4 Sprinkle with a little more flour and bake for 45 mins–1 hr or until the bread is risen, golden and, if you tap the crust with your knuckles, it sounds hollow.

5 Turn the bread out onto a wire rack and leave to cool for 10–15 mins before slicing. Delicious served warm with olive oil, balsamic vinegar and sea salt flakes. Will freeze whole or in slices.

Nutrition per slice (12)
kcal 162 • fat 2g • saturates 0g • carbs 29g • sugars 0g • fibre 1g • protein 5g • salt 0.8g

Simnel share 'n' tear buns

Don't choose between hot cross buns, Simnel cake and Chelsea buns – this ingenious bake brings together all three.

MORE EFFORT ⏱ PREP 1 hr 30 mins plus rising and proving COOK 30 mins ⏲ MAKES 12 LITTLE BUNS

- 300g strong white bread flour
- 140g plain flour, plus extra for dusting
- 50g golden caster sugar
- 7g sachet fast-action dried yeast
- zest 1 lemon
- 200ml warm milk
- 2 tsp almond extract
- 1 large egg
- oil, for greasing bowl/ proving

FOR THE FILLING
- 50g butter, at room temperature
- 100g light soft brown sugar
- 2 tsp mixed spice
- 1 tbsp lemon juice
- 50g mixed peel
- 50g currants
- 50g marzipan, coarsely grated, plus 50g extra for the 'Apostle' balls

TO FINISH
- 85g apricot jam
- 85g icing sugar, sifted
- 2 tbsp toasted flaked almonds

1 Mix the flours, sugar, yeast, zest and 1 tsp salt in a big bowl. In a separate bowl, whisk together the milk, almond extract and egg, then stir into the dry ingredients with a cutlery knife. Leave to rest for 10 mins.

2 Knead the dough for 10 mins on a lightly floured surface until smooth and no longer sticky, then put in an oiled bowl, cover with oiled cling film and leave to rise somewhere warm-ish for at least 1 hr until doubled in size.

3 Line the base of a 25 x 35cm tin, or 30cm square, with baking parchment. Mix the first 4 filling ingredients to a smooth paste, then stir in the dried fruit and 50g marzipan.

4 Roll out the dough to a rectangle about 35 x 25cm. Crumble over the filling and press into the dough. Roll up tightly from one long side and, using a floured knife, cut into 12 even pieces. Put these into the tin, spiral-side up, leaving 0.5cm space between them. Cover with oiled cling film and leave to rise for 30–45 mins until nearly doubled in size.

5 Heat oven to 200C/180C fan/gas 6. Bake the buns for 25–30 mins. If they are browning too quickly after 15 mins, cover loosely with baking parchment. Take the buns out of the oven and, while warm, melt the jam and brush all over the top. Leave to cool in the tin. Once cool, mix the icing sugar with a little water to a runny consistency and drizzle over. With the remaining marzipan, make 11 balls to represent the Apostles – without Judas – and scatter over with the almonds. Best eaten the day of baking. If making ahead or freezing, warm through in a low oven before serving to give that just-baked flavour.

Nutrition per bun
kcal 340 • fat 7g • saturates 3g • carbs 62g • sugars 35g • fibre 2g • protein 7g • salt 0.2g

Monkey bread

This American, pull-apart sweet treat is sticky, spiced and stuffed with pecans – an indulgent breakfast, brunch or dessert to share.

EASY ⏱ PREP 1 hr 15 mins plus rising and proving COOK 35 mins ◷ SERVES 12

FOR THE DOUGH
- 200ml semi-skimmed milk
- 85g unsalted butter
- 2 large eggs
- 550g strong white bread flour, plus extra for kneading if doing it by hand
- 2½ tsp fast-action dried yeast
- 50g golden caster sugar
- oil, for greasing

TO ASSEMBLE
- 125g unsalted butter, plus extra for greasing
- 1 tbsp ground cinnamon
- 1 tsp ground ginger
- 1 tsp ground nutmeg
- 225g light muscovado sugar
- 140g pecans, toasted then roughly chopped

FOR THE GLAZE
- 100g icing sugar, sifted
- ½ tsp vanilla extract
- 1 tbsp semi-skimmed milk
- pinch of ground cinnamon
- 2 tbsp unsalted butter, melted

1 Start with the dough. Put the milk and butter into a medium pan and heat gently until the butter melts and the milk is at a simmer. Cool for a few mins, then beat in the eggs with a fork. Mix the dry ingredients in a large bowl with 1½ tsp fine salt, then add the liquid and stir to a sticky dough. Leave for 5 mins, then tip onto a floured worktop and knead for 5–10 mins until smooth and springy. Use a little oil to grease a large bowl, add the dough, turn it in the oil to coat, then cover the bowl with cling film. Leave in a warm place for 1 hr or until doubled in size. Knead in a tabletop mixer with a dough hook if you prefer.

2 To assemble, grease a 25cm bundt pan with butter. Melt the rest of the butter in a pan. In a bowl mix the spices, sugar and pinch of salt. Spoon 2 tbsp melted butter, 3 tbsp spiced sugar and 4 tbsp pecans into the bottom of the tin.

3 Pull the dough into about 65 small pieces and roll into balls. Taking 4 or 5 at a time, dunk the dough balls into the melted butter, let the excess drain off, then tip them into the spiced sugar. Roll to coat, then put haphazardly into the tin. Repeat until there's a full layer of dough in the tin. Scatter with the rest of the chopped nuts, then carry on filling the tin with the coated dough balls. Tip any leftover sugar and butter over the dough. Can be frozen now for up to 1 month. Defrost in the fridge then let prove.

4 Cover the pan with oiled clingfilm then leave to rise in a warm place for 1 hr, or until risen and the dough no longer springs back when you poke it.

5 Heat the oven to 180C/160C fan/gas 4. Bake the monkey bread for 35 mins, or until well risen and golden. Let the pan cool for 5 mins, then give it a sharp rap on the counter. Leave in the tin until just warm.

6 Whisk all of the ingredients together to make the glaze. It will thicken as the melted butter cools. Turn the bread onto a plate, then drizzle with the glaze. Let it set.

Nutrition per serving
kcal 546 • fat 27g • saturates 12g • carbs 65g • sugars 32g • fibre 2g • protein 9g • salt 0.7g

Brummie bacon cakes

These brunch cakes from Birmingham are similar to savoury scones, with cheese, tomato ketchup and Worcester sauce – perfect with eggs.

MORE EFFORT ⏱ PREP 15 mins COOK 40 mins ⏲ SERVES 4

- 3 rashers streaky bacon (we used smoked)
- 225g self-raising flour, plus extra for dusting
- 25g butter, cold and cut into small pieces
- 75g mature cheddar, grated
- 150ml milk, plus 2 tbsp extra for glazing
- 1 tbsp tomato ketchup
- ½ tsp Worcestershire sauce

1 Heat grill to high and grill the bacon for 10 mins, turning halfway, until crisp. Cool for a few mins. Meanwhile, heat oven to 180C/160C fan/gas 4 and line a baking sheet with parchment. Sift the flour and ½ tsp salt into a bowl, add the butter, then rub in to the texture of fine breadcrumbs. Cut the bacon into small pieces and add to the bowl with a third of the cheese.

2 Mix the milk, ketchup and Worcestershire sauce in a jug. Pour into the bacon mixture, stirring briefly, to make a soft dough. Flour the work surface, turn the dough onto it and shape into an 18cm round. Brush with milk, then cut into 8 wedges with a large knife.

3 Arrange the wedges on the baking sheet and sprinkle with the remaining cheese.

4 Bake for 20–30 mins or until risen and golden brown, and serve warm (or cool on a wire rack, and store in an airtight container or freeze). Warm the bacon cakes through in a low oven (140C/120C fan/gas 1) if you've made them in advance.

Nutrition per serving
kcal 395 • fat 17g • saturates 9g • carbs 44g • sugars 4g • fibre 2g • protein 15g • salt 2.1g

Homemade crumpets with burnt honey butter

Light, fluffy, fresh crumpets are perfect for a weekend brunch – top with sweet and salty burnt honey butter.

MORE EFFORT ⏱ PREP 20 mins plus rising COOK 20 mins ⏲ SERVES 4

- 250ml milk
- 200g plain flour
- 1 tsp fast-action dried yeast
- 1 tsp golden caster sugar
- 2 tbsp vegetable oil, plus extra for greasing

FOR THE BURNT HONEY BUTTER
- 5 tbsp clear honey
- 140g unsalted butter, at room temperature

1 Gently heat the milk in a small pan until it starts to bubble around the edges, then leave it to cool until it is tepid. Put the flour, yeast, sugar and ½ tsp fine salt in a large bowl, and gradually mix in the cooled milk to make a smooth, loose batter. Cover and leave to rise in a warm place for 1hr-1hr 30 mins or until doubled in size and very bubbly.

2 Meanwhile, make the honey butter. Heat the honey in a small saucepan over a medium-high heat. Let it bubble until it turns to a deep gold, then remove and cool slightly. Using electric beaters or a wooden spoon, beat the butter in a large bowl until fluffy and pale, add a large pinch of sea salt, then fold in the warm honey. Scrape into a serving bowl and chill. Can be made a day ahead.

3 When the batter has risen, heat the grill to high. Lightly grease the insides of 4 x 9cm metal cooks' rings with oil. Heat a large non-stick frying pan over a low-medium heat, add 1 tbsp oil and put the rings in the pan. Spoon the batter into the rings until they are half full. Let the crumpets cook slowly for about 10 mins or until the mixture has set and the bubbles on top have all popped. Lift the rings away carefully. If your pan has a heatproof handle, grill the crumpets in the pan for 7–10 mins or until the tops are golden brown. If not, transfer to a baking sheet and grill them on that instead. Can be made up to a day ahead or frozen.

4 Warm through in an oven at 140C/120C fan/gas 1 if you've made them in advance. Repeat with the remaining mix, then serve with the burnt honey butter.

Nutrition per serving
kcal 609 • fat 36g • saturates 19g • carbs 63g • sugars 26g • fibre 2g • protein 2g • salt 0.7g

Toasted banana bread with vanilla ricotta & raspberries

This classic banana bread is best baked the day before – topped with a fruity compote, it makes a lovely sweet brunch or light dessert.

MORE EFFORT ⏱ PREP 30 mins COOK 1 hr 10 mins ⏲ SERVES 8

FOR THE BANANA BREAD
- 140g butter, softened
- 140g light muscovado sugar
- 2 large eggs
- 2–3 very ripe bananas
- zest ½ lemon
- 1 tsp vanilla bean paste
- 85g buttermilk
- 225g self-raising flour
- 1 tsp ground cinnamon
- ½ tsp bicarbonate of soda

FOR THE VANILLA RICOTTA
- 250g tub ricotta
- 3 tsp vanilla bean paste
- juice 2 oranges, 1 zested

FOR THE RASPBERRY COMPOTE
- zest and juice 2 oranges
- 85g granulated sugar
- 600g raspberries

1 Heat oven to 160C/140C fan/gas 3. Grease and line the base of a 900g loaf tin with baking parchment. Beat together the butter and sugar until light and fluffy, then beat in the eggs, one at a time. In a separate bowl, mash the bananas with a fork, add to the bowl with the lemon zest, vanilla and buttermilk, and stir.

2 Mix together the flour, cinnamon and bicarbonate of soda. Fold into the banana mix, one-third at a time, until just combined and add to the tin. Bake for 1 hr until firm, golden brown and a skewer inserted into the centre comes out clean. Leave in the tin for 10 mins, then turn out onto a wire rack to cool completely. If you want to freeze the loaf at this point then cool it first.

3 While the banana bread is baking, make the vanilla ricotta. Tip the ricotta into a bowl and mix with the vanilla bean paste, orange zest and 90ml orange juice until just combined. Cover and chill.

4 To make the raspberry compote, heat the orange zest, 5 tbsp orange juice, the sugar and 225g of the raspberries in a saucepan over a gentle heat until the sugar has dissolved. Simmer for 5 mins, then pour through a sieve into a bowl. Stir through the rest of the raspberries, cover and chill.

5 When you are ready to serve, take the raspberry compote out of the fridge to bring to room temperature. Slice the banana bread into 8 pieces and toast under a medium grill until lightly caramelised. Serve each slice with a spoonful of vanilla ricotta and a drizzle of raspberry compote.

Nutrition per serving
kcal 483 • fat 20g • saturates 12g • carbs 63g • sugars 42g • fibre 4g • protein 9g • salt 0.9g

Croissants

James Martin shares his recipe for this French patisserie classic. It involves some ambitious pastry work, but the end results are worth it.

A CHALLENGE ⏱ PREP 1 hr 15 mins plus overnight chilling COOK 15 mins ⏲ MAKES 12–14

- 500g strong white flour, plus extra for dusting
- 1½ tsp salt
- 50g sugar
- 2 x 7g sachets fast-action dried yeast
- oil, for greasing
- 300g butter, at room temperature
- 1 egg, beaten

1 Put the flour, salt and sugar in a bowl. Measure 300ml cold water, add the yeast and stir. Make a well in the flour and pour in the liquid. Mix, then knead for 10 mins. Shape into a ball, put in a lightly oiled bowl, cover and chill for 2 hrs.

2 Put the butter between 2 sheets of baking parchment. Using a rolling pin, bash and roll it into a 20 x 15cm rectangle. Leave wrapped in the parchment and chill.

3 Transfer the chilled dough to a floured surface and roll into a 40 x 20cm rectangle. Place the unwrapped slab of butter in the centre of the dough so that it covers the middle third.

4 Fold one side of the dough up and halfway over the butter. Fold the other side of the dough up and over the butter in the same way, so that the two edges of the dough meet in the centre of the butter. Fold the dough in half so that the point where the ends meet becomes the seam. Wrap in cling film and chill for 30 mins. Repeat the rolling, folding and chilling process twice more in exactly the same way – rolling the pastry while it's still folded – without adding more butter. Wrap and chill overnight.

5 The next day, roll the dough out on a floured surface into a 60 x 30cm rectangle. Using a knife, trim the edges.

6 Cut the dough in half lengthways so you have 2 long strips, then cut each strip into 6 or 7 triangles with 2 equal sides.

7 Take each triangle in turn and pull the 2 corners at the base to stretch and widen it. Starting at the base of each triangle, gently roll into a croissant. Continue rolling, making sure the tip of each triangle ends up tucked under the croissant to hold in place. Bend the ends of the croissants inwards, then transfer to baking trays lined with baking parchment, spaced well apart. Can be frozen at this point; defrost and then continue with the recipe. Cover with oiled cling film and leave to rise for 2 hrs, or until doubled in size.

8 Heat oven to 200C/180C fan/gas 6. Mix the egg with a pinch of salt and use to generously glaze the croissants. Bake for 15–18 mins until risen and golden brown, then cool on a wire rack.

Nutrition per croissant (14)
kcal 310 • fat 19g • saturates 11g • carbs 29g • sugars 4g • fibre 1g • protein 5g • salt 0.9g

Fig, nut & seed bread with ricotta & fruit

Start the day well with this fruit and nut breakfast loaf, spread with cream cheese and topped with orange or apple. It keeps for a month, too.

EASY 🕐 PREP 15 mins COOK 1 hr 15 mins 🕑 CUTS INTO 16 SLICES

- 400ml hot strong black tea
- 100g dried figs, hard stalks removed, thinly sliced
- 140g sultanas
- 50g porridge oats
- 200g self-raising wholemeal flour
- 1 tsp baking powder
- 100g mixed nuts (almonds, walnuts, Brazils, hazelnuts), plus 50g for the topping
- 1 tbsp golden linseed
- 1 tbsp sesame seeds, plus 2 tsp to sprinkle
- 25g pumpkin seeds
- 1 large egg

TO SERVE
- 25g ricotta per person
- 1 orange or green apple, thickly sliced, per person

1 Heat oven to 170C/150C fan/gas 3½. Pour the tea into a large bowl and stir in the figs, sultanas and oats. Set aside to soak.

2 Meanwhile, line the base and sides of a 1kg loaf tin with baking parchment. Mix together the flour, baking powder, nuts and seeds. Beat the egg into the cooled fruit mixture, then stir the dry ingredients into the wet. Pour into the tin, then level the top and scatter with the extra nuts and sesame seeds.

3 Bake for 1 hr, then cover the top with foil and bake for 15 mins more until a skewer inserted into the centre of the loaf comes out clean. Remove from the tin to cool, but leave the parchment on until cold. Cut into slices, spread with ricotta and serve with fruit. Will keep in the fridge for 1 month, or freeze in slices.

Nutrition per serving (1 slice with ricotta and fruit)
kcal 249 • fat 10g • saturates 3g • carbs 30g • sugars 20g • fibre 6g • protein 10g • salt 0.3g

Blueberry & seed breakfast muffins

Make muffins healthier with mashed banana and apple sauce for natural sweetness, plus blueberries and seeds for an extra nutritious hit.

EASY ⏲ PREP 15 mins COOK 30 mins ⏲ MAKES 12

- 2 large eggs
- 150ml pot natural low-fat yogurt
- 50ml rapeseed oil
- 100g apple sauce or puréed apples (find with the baby food)
- 1 ripe banana, mashed
- 4 tbsp clear honey
- 1 tsp vanilla extract
- 200g wholemeal flour
- 50g rolled oats, plus extra for sprinkling
- 1½ tsp baking powder
- 1½ tsp bicarbonate of soda
- 1½ tsp cinnamon
- 100g blueberries
- 2 tbsp mixed seed (we used pumpkin, sunflower and flaxseed)

1 Heat oven to 180C/160C fan/gas 4. Line a 12-hole muffin tin with 12 large muffin cases. In a jug, mix the eggs, yogurt, oil, apple sauce, banana, honey and vanilla. Tip the remaining ingredients, except the seeds, into a large bowl, add a pinch of salt and mix to combine.

2 Pour the wet ingredients into the dry and mix briefly until you have a smooth batter – don't overmix as this will make the muffins heavy. Divide the batter among the cases. Sprinkle the muffins with the extra oats and the seeds. Bake for 25–30 mins until golden and well risen, and a skewer inserted into the centre of a muffin comes out clean. Remove from the oven, transfer to a wire rack and leave to cool. Can be stored in a sealed container for up to 3 days or frozen.

Nutrition per muffin
kcal 179 • fat 7g • saturates 1g • carbs 23g • sugars 10g • fibre 3g • protein 5g • salt 0.6g

Raspberry, chocolate & hazelnut breakfast bread

This indulgent brunch loaf requires good bread and kneading skills. Prepare the dough ahead then pop it in the oven to serve warm.

MORE EFFORT 🕐 PREP 1 hr plus overnight (or up to 3 days) chilling COOK 30 mins 🕒 SERVES 8-10

- 2 x 7g sachets fast-action dried yeast
- 600g '00' flour, sponge flour or plain flour, plus extra for dusting
- 50g golden caster sugar
- 400ml warm milk
- 50g melted salted butter, plus extra for greasing and to serve
- 1 large egg, beaten
- 200g jar Nutella, plus extra to serve (optional)
- 200g raspberries
- 1–2 tbsp chopped hazelnuts
- 1 tbsp granulated sugar
- raspberry jam, to serve

1 Up to 3 days before you want to bake (and best if at least 1 day), mix the yeast, 400g of the flour, the sugar and 1 tsp salt in a big bowl. Whisk together the milk, melted butter and egg, then tip into the dry ingredients and mix with a wooden spoon. Cover tightly with greased cling film and chill at least overnight or up to 3 days. Can be frozen; defrost before proving.

2 When you're ready to finish the bread, heat oven to 180C/160C fan/gas 4. Add the remaining flour to the dough and use your hands to mix in. Tip onto a lightly floured surface and lightly knead to completely bring together. Roll out with a little more flour to a 50 x 30cm rectangle. Spread the Nutella all over the dough. Scatter the raspberries evenly over, then press lightly with your hands so they stick into the dough a bit.

3 With a long side facing you, roll up as tightly as you can (like a Swiss roll). Use a sharp knife, dusted with a little flour, to cut the roll in half down the length – but not quite through at one end, so the 2 strips are still joined. Twist the 2 strips together, then bring the ends together to make a wreath, pinching the ends together to stick. Lift onto a baking sheet, scatter with the hazelnuts and granulated sugar, and bake for 30–40 mins until browned and crusty. Cool until just warm. Serve with butter, raspberry jam and extra Nutella, if you like.

Nutrition per serving (10)
kcal 422 • fat 14g • saturates 6g • carbs 64g • sugars 22g • fibre 4g • protein 10g • salt 0.7g

Blueberry & lemon pancakes

Get your kids to help prepare a batch of American-style pancakes – the zesty berry topping makes these a healthy brunch option.

EASY 🕐 PREP 10 mins COOK 20 mins 🕐 MAKES 14-16

- 200g plain flour
- 1 tsp cream of tartar
- ½ tsp bicarbonate of soda
- 1 tsp golden syrup
- 75g blueberries
- zest 1 lemon
- 200ml milk
- 1 large egg
- butter, for cooking

1 First, put the flour, cream of tartar and bicarbonate of soda in a bowl. Mix them well with a fork. Drop the golden syrup into the dry ingredients along with the blueberries and lemon zest.

2 Pour the milk into a measuring jug. Now break in the egg and mix well with a fork. Pour most of the milk mixture into the bowl and mix well with a rubber spatula. Keep adding more milk until you get a smooth, thick, pouring batter.

3 Heat the frying pan and brush with a little butter. Then spoon in the batter, 1 tbsp at a time, in heaps. Bubbles will appear on top as the pancakes cook – turn them at this stage, using a metal spatula to help you. Cook until brown on the second side, then keep warm on a plate, covered with foil. Repeat until all the mixture is used up. Can be cooled and frozen; separate pancakes with squares of baking parchment to stop them sticking.

Nutrition per pancake (14)
kcal 69 • fat 1g • saturates 1g • carbs 12g • sugars 2g • fibre 1g • protein 2g • salt 0.1g

Summer fruit compote

Add summer raspberries, blueberries and juicy plums to orange juice for a nutritious breakfast mix.

EASY 🕐 PREP 5 mins COOK 10 mins 🕐 SERVES 4

- 4 large plums, stoned and cut into wedges
- 200g punnet blueberries
- zest and juice 1 orange
- 25g soft light brown sugar
- 150g punnet raspberries
- thick yogurt and honey, to serve (optional)

1 Cook the plums and blueberries in a small pan with the orange zest and juice, sugar and 4 tbsp water until slightly softened but not mushy. Gently stir in the raspberries and cook for 1 min more.

2 Remove from the heat and allow to cool to room temperature. Freeze at this point; defrost in the fridge. Serve with yogurt and a drizzle of honey, if you like.

Nutrition per serving
kcal 98 • fat 0g • saturates 0g • carbs 22g • sugars 21g • fibre 4g • protein 2g • salt 0g

Healthy veggie ragu

Struggling to get your 5-a-day? This superhealthy ragu will get you 4 steps closer and the sauce can be frozen for extra convenience.

EASY 🕐 PREP 15 mins COOK 1 hr 15 mins 🕐 SERVES 6

- 3 tbsp olive oil
- 2 onions, finely chopped
- 3 carrots, finely chopped
- 3 celery sticks, finely chopped
- 3 garlic cloves, crushed
- 500g bag dried red lentils
- 2 x 400g cans chopped tomatoes
- 2 tbsp tomato purée
- 2 tsp each dried oregano and thyme
- 3 bay leaves
- 1 litre vegetable stock
- 500g spaghetti
- Parmesan or vegetarian cheese, grated, to serve

1 Heat the oil in a large saucepan and add the onions, carrots, celery and garlic. Cook gently for 15–20 mins until everything is softened. Stir in the lentils, chopped tomatoes, tomato purée, herbs and stock. Bring to a simmer, then cook for 40–50 mins until the lentils are tender and saucy – splash in water if you need. Season.

2 If eating straight away, keep on a low heat while you cook the spaghetti, following pack instructions. Drain well, divide among pasta bowls or plates, spoon sauce over the top and grate over cheese. If eating later, chill for up to 3 days or freeze for up to 3 months in freezerproof containers. Simply defrost portions overnight at room temperature, then reheat gently to serve.

Nutrition per serving
kcal 662 • protein 33g • carbs 120g • fat 9g • saturates 1g • fibre 10g • sugar 14g • salt 1.05g

Italian vegetable soup

Warm up your week with this good-for-you vegetable soup that's easy to freeze ahead.

EASY ⏱ PREP 15 mins COOK 30 mins 🕐 SERVES 8

- 2 each of onions and carrots, chopped
- 4 sticks celery, chopped
- 1 tbsp olive oil
- 2 tbsp sugar
- 4 garlic cloves, crushed
- 2 tbsp tomato purée
- 2 bay leaves
- few sprigs thyme
- 3 courgettes, chopped
- 400g can butter beans, drained
- 400g can chopped tomatoes
- 1.2 litres vegetable stock
- 100g Parmesan or vegetarian cheese, grated
- 140g small pasta shapes
- small bunch basil, shredded

1 Gently cook the onion, carrots and celery in the oil in a large saucepan for 20 mins, until soft. Splash in water if they stick. Add the sugar, garlic, tomato purée, herbs and courgettes and cook for 4–5 mins on a medium heat until they brown a little.

2 Pour in the beans, tomatoes and stock, then simmer for 20 mins. If you're freezing it, cool and do so now. Freeze in freezerproof containers. If not, add half the Parmesan and the pasta and simmer for 6–8 mins until pasta cooked. Sprinkle with basil and the remaining Parmesan to serve. If frozen, defrost then re-heat before adding pasta and cheese and continuing as above.

Nutrition per serving
kcal 215 • fat 6g • saturates 3g • carbs 30g • sugars 12g • fibre 5g • protein 11g • salt 1.06g

Rustic vegetable soup

This vegetarian soup is packed with vegetables and lentils – it's healthy, low fat and full of flavour. To bulk it up, why not add borlotti beans or chicken?

EASY PREP 15 mins COOK 30 mins SERVES 4

- 1 tbsp rapeseed oil
- 1 large onion, chopped
- 2 carrots, chopped
- 2 celery sticks, chopped
- 50g dried red lentils
- 1.5 litres boiling vegetable bouillon (we used Marigold)
- 2 tbsp tomato purée
- 1 tbsp chopped thyme
- 1 leek, finely sliced
- 175g bite-sized cauliflower florets
- 1 courgette, chopped
- 3 garlic cloves, finely chopped
- ½ large Savoy cabbage, stalks removed and leaves chopped
- 1 tbsp basil, chopped

1 Heat the oil in a large pan with a lid. Add the onion, carrots and celery and fry for 10 mins, stirring from time to time until they are starting to colour a little around the edges. Stir in the lentils and cook for 1 min more.

2 Pour in the hot bouillon, add the tomato purée and thyme and stir well. Add the leek, cauliflower, courgette and garlic, bring to the boil, then cover and leave to simmer for 15 mins.

3 Add the cabbage and basil and cook for 5 mins more until the veg is just tender. Season with pepper, ladle into bowls and serve. Will keep in the fridge for a couple of days. Freezes well. Thaw, then reheat in a pan until piping hot.

Nutrition per serving
kcal 162 • fat 5g • saturates 1g • carbs 19g • sugars 9g • fibre 7g • protein 7g • salt 0.4g

Double bean & roasted pepper chilli

This warming vegetarian chilli is a low-fat, healthy option that packs in the veggies and flavour. Serve with Tabasco sauce, soured cream or yogurt.

EASY   PREP 30 mins COOK 1 hr 15 mins   SERVES 8

- 2 onions, chopped
- 2 celery sticks, finely chopped
- 2 yellow or orange peppers, finely chopped
- 2 tbsp rapeseed or sunflower oil
- 2 x 460g jars roasted red peppers
- 2 tsp chipotle paste
- 2 tbsp red wine vinegar
- 1 tbsp each cocoa powder, dried oregano and sweet smoked paprika
- 2 tbsp ground cumin
- 1 tsp ground cinnamon
- 2 x 400g cans chopped tomatoes
- 400g can refried beans
- 3 x 400g cans kidney beans, drained and rinsed
- 2 x 400g cans black beans, drained and rinsed

1. Put the onions, celery and chopped peppers with the oil in your largest flameproof casserole dish or heavy-based saucepan, and fry gently over a low heat until soft but not coloured.
2. Drain both jars of peppers over a bowl to catch the juices. Put a quarter of the peppers into a food processor with the chipotle paste, vinegar, cocoa, dried spices and herbs. Whizz to a purée, then stir into the softened veg and cook for a few mins.
3. Add the tomatoes and refried beans with 1 can water and the reserved pepper juice. Simmer for 1 hr until thickened, smoky and the tomato chunks have broken down to a smoother sauce.
4. At this stage you can cool and chill or freeze the sauce if making ahead. Otherwise add the kidney and black beans, and the remaining roasted peppers, cut into bite-sized pieces, then reheat. (This makes a large batch, so once the sauce is ready it might be easier to split it between 2 pans when you add the beans and peppers.) Once bubbling and the beans are hot, season to taste and serve.

Nutrition per serving
kcal 327 • fat 6g • saturates 1g • carbs 41g • sugars 9g • fibre 18g • protein 19g • salt 0.6g

Tofu & spinach cannelloni

Tasty tofu is a vegetarian's best friend and this cannelloni dish, packed with protein and iron is sure to be a freezable favourite.

EASY ⏱ PREP 25 mins COOK 1 hr ⏳ SERVES 6

- 2 tbsp olive oil
- 1 onion, chopped
- 3 garlic cloves, finely chopped
- 2 x 400g cans chopped tomatoes
- 50g pine nuts, roughly chopped
- 400g bag spinach
- pinch grated nutmeg
- 349g pack silken tofu
- 300g pack fresh lasagne sheets
- 4 tbsp fresh breadcrumbs

1 Heat half the oil in a pan, add the onion and a third of the garlic and fry for 4 mins until softened. Pour in the tomatoes, season and bring to the boil. Reduce the heat and cook for 10 mins until the sauce thickens.

2 Heat half remaining oil in a frying pan and cook another third of garlic for 1 min, then add half the pine nuts and the spinach. Wilt the spinach, then tip out excess liquid. Whizz the tofu in a food processor or with a hand blender until smooth, then stir through the spinach with the nutmeg and some pepper. Remove from the heat; allow to cool slightly.

3 Heat oven to 200C/180C fan/gas 6. Pour half the tomato sauce into a 20 x 30cm dish. Divide the spinach mix among the lasagne sheets, roll up and lay on top of the sauce. Pour over the remaining sauce. Bake for 30 mins. You can freeze the dish before or after baking and cook from frozen, but make sure the centre of the dish is cooked through; it should take another 10 minutes or so.

4 Mix the crumbs with the remaining garlic and pine nuts. Sprinkle over the top of the dish, drizzle with the remaining oil and bake for 10 mins until the crumbs are golden.

Nutrition per serving
kcal 284 • fat 13g • saturates 2g • carbs 30g • sugars 6g • fibre 4g • protein 13g • salt 0.65g

Mexican bean soup with shredded chicken & lime

Use leftover chicken breast in this substantial healthy soup. Alternatively, make the recipe vegetarian by topping with chunky, fresh guacamole. You can make and freeze the base so you have it to hand when you've leftovers from a roast chicken.

EASY 🕐 PREP 10 mins COOK 20 mins 🕒 SERVES 2

- 2 tsp rapeseed oil
- 1 large onion, finely chopped
- 1 red pepper, cut into chunks
- 2 garlic cloves, chopped
- 2 tsp mild chilli powder
- 1 tsp ground coriander
- 1 tsp ground cumin
- 400g can chopped tomatoes
- 400g can black beans
- 1 tsp vegetable bouillon powder
- 1 cooked skinless chicken breast, about 125g, shredded
- handful chopped coriander
- 1 lime, juiced
- ½ red chilli, deseeded and finely chopped (optional)

1 Heat the oil in a medium pan, add the onion and pepper, and fry, stirring frequently, for 10 mins. Stir in the garlic and spices, then tip in the tomatoes and beans with their liquid, half a can of water and the bouillon powder. Simmer, covered, for 15 mins. The base can be frozen at this point; bring back to a simmer to continue the recipe.

2 Meanwhile, tip the chicken into a bowl, add the coriander and lime juice with a little chilli (if using) and toss well. Ladle the soup into two bowls, top with the chicken and serve.

Nutrition: per serving
kcal 378 • fat 8g • saturates 1g • carbs 36g • sugars 17g • fibre 12g • protein 32g • salt 0.5g

Red lentil, chickpea & chilli soup

Come home to a warming bowlful of this filling, low-fat soup.

EASY ⏱ PREP 10 mins COOK 25 mins 🕒 SERVES 4

- 2 tsp cumin seeds
- large pinch chilli flakes
- 1 tbsp olive oil
- 1 red onion, chopped
- 140g red split lentils
- 850ml vegetable stock or water
- 400g can tomatoes, whole or chopped
- 200g can chickpeas or ½ a can, rinsed and drained (freeze leftovers)
- small bunch coriander, roughly chopped (save a few leaves, to serve)
- 4 tbsp 0% Greek yogurt, to serve

1 Heat a large saucepan and dry-fry the cumin seeds and chilli flakes for 1 min, or until they start to jump around the pan and release their aromas. Add the oil and onion, and cook for 5 mins. Stir in the lentils, stock and tomatoes, then bring to the boil. Simmer for 15 mins until the lentils have softened.

2 Whizz the soup with a stick blender or in a food processor until it is a rough purée, pour back into the pan and add the chickpeas. If freezing, cool and portion into freezerproof containers. To serve, heat gently, season well and stir in the coriander. Finish with a dollop of yogurt and coriander leaves.

Nutrition per serving
Kcals 222 • 5g fat • 0g saturates • 33g carbs • 6g sugars • 6g fibre • 13g protein • 0.87g salt

Mexican bean soup with shredded chicken & lime (or veggie version with guac)

Use leftover chicken breast in this substantial healthy soup. You could make a veggie version by topping the soup with guacamole instead of chicken: mash a small avocado with lime and fresh chilli, then stir in a chopped tomato, a tablespoon of finely chopped onion and fresh coriander.

EASY soup only ⏱ PREP 10 mins COOK 20 mins ◷ SERVES 2

- 2 tsp rapeseed oil
- 1 large onion, finely chopped
- 1 red pepper, cut into chunks
- 2 garlic cloves, chopped
- 2 tsp mild chilli powder
- 1 tsp each ground coriander and ground cumin
- 400g can chopped tomatoes
- 400g can black beans
- 1 tsp vegetable bouillon powder
- 1 cooked skinless chicken breast, about 125g, shredded
- handful chopped coriander
- 1 lime, juiced
- 1/2 red chilli, deseeded and finely chopped (optional)

1 Heat the oil in a medium pan, add the onion and pepper, and fry, stirring frequently, for 10 mins. Stir in the garlic and spices, then tip in the tomatoes and beans with their liquid, half a can of water and the bouillon powder. Simmer, covered, for 15 mins. *Freeze the base at this point and bring it back to a simmer when you need it.*

2 Meanwhile, tip the chicken into a bowl, add the coriander and lime juice with a little chilli (if using) and toss well. Ladle the soup into two bowls, top with the chicken and serve.

Nutrition per serving
378 kcal • fat 8g • saturates 1g • carbs 36g • sugars 17g • fibre 12g • protein 32g • salt 0.5g

Smoky beef stew

Enjoy this simple stew for dinner, then pack into boxes to keep you going for lunches.

EASY ⏱ PREP 10 mins COOK 3 hrs ⏳ MAKES 6-8 PORTIONS

- 1kg stewing beef, cut into large chunks
- 2 onions, chopped
- 2 x 400g cans chopped tomatoes
- 2 tsp each sweet paprika, ground cumin and mild chilli powder
- 2 tbsp red or white vinegar
- 2 tbsp caster sugar
- 400g can butter beans, rinsed and drained

1 Heat oven to 160C/140C fan/gas 3. Mix the beef, onions, tomatoes, spices, vinegar and sugar in a casserole dish. Cover and bake for 2½ hrs. Stir in the beans and bake for 30 mins more (with the lid off if the casserole is a little wet or lid on if a good consistency), until the beef is tender.
2 Cool, then freeze in 6–8 portions in small food bags or plastic containers. Defrost in the microwave or overnight in fridge, then heat in the morning and transfer to a thermos container, or heat in the microwave at lunchtime.

Nutrition per serving (6)
kcal 341 • fat 12g • saturates 5g • carbs 18g • sugars 11g • fibre 4g • protein 42g • salt 0.92g

Beef & swede casserole

This gluten and dairy-free casserole is hearty and comforting, packed with chunky meat and veg. Simple to prepare, just serve up with seasonal greens.

EASY ⏱ PREP 15 mins COOK 1 hr 25 mins 🕒 SERVES 4

- 2 tbsp vegetable oil
- 2 onions, sliced
- ½ celery stick, sliced
- 500g diced braising beef
- 200ml red wine (optional)
- 700ml beef (or chicken) stock
- 500g swede, peeled and cut into chunky dice
- 300g floury potatoes (such as Maris Piper), diced
- 3 thyme sprigs
- 1 bay leaf
- green veg, to serve (optional)

1 Heat the oil in a flameproof casserole dish over a medium-high heat. Fry the onions and celery for a few mins until turning brown. Add the beef and brown all over for 3–4 mins. Pour in the wine, if using, and let it reduce by half. Add the stock and toss in the swede, potatoes, thyme and bay leaf. Season and bring to the boil.

2 Reduce the heat, cover with a lid and leave for 1 hr. If you want to reduce the liquid a little, remove the lid, turn up the heat and cook for a further 10–15 mins or until the sauce has thickened.

3 Season to taste and remove the thyme sprigs and bay leaf. Serve with some green veg, if you like. Freeze any leftovers in a freezer bag.

Nutrition per serving
kcal 352 • fat 15g • saturates 4g • carbs 20g • sugars 7g • fibre 5g • protein 30g • salt 0.6g

Courgette, potato & cheddar soup

This freezable soup is a delicious way to use up a glut of courgettes.

EASY ⏱ PREP 15 mins COOK 15 mins ⏲ SERVES 8

- 500g potatoes, unpeeled and roughly chopped
- 2 vegetable stock cubes
- 1kg courgettes, roughly chopped
- bunch spring onions, sliced – save 1 for serving, if eating straight away
- 100g extra-mature cheddar or vegetarian alternative, grated, plus a little extra to serve
- good grating fresh nutmeg, plus extra to serve

1 Put the potatoes in a large pan with just enough water to cover them and crumble in the stock cubes. Bring to the boil, then cover and cook for 5 mins. Add the courgettes, put the lid back on and cook for 5 mins more. Throw in the spring onions, cover and cook for a final 5 mins.

2 Take off the heat, then stir in the cheese and season with the nutmeg, salt and pepper. Whizz to a thick soup, adding more hot water until you get the consistency you like. Serve scattered with extra grated cheddar, spring onions and nutmeg or pepper. Alternatively, cool and freeze in freezer bags or containers with good lids for up to 3 months.

Nutrition per serving
kcal 131 • fat 6g • saturates 3g • carbs 14g • sugars 3g • fibre 2g • protein 7g • salt 1.31g

Creamy prawn & spring vegetable pot

Packed with goodness, this freeze-ahead one-pot is quick to prepare and counts towards your 5-a-day.

EASY ⏱ PREP 10 mins COOK 30 mins ⏲ SERVES 8

- 850ml low-salt chicken or vegetable stock
- 100g pearl barley
- 750g new potatoes, sliced
- ½ spring cabbage, shredded
- 140g frozen broad or soya beans
- 100g frozen peas
- 250g broccoli florets
- 200g tub crème fraîche
- small bunch dill, snipped
- zest 1 lemon, plus squeeze of juice
- 600g cooked, peeled prawns

1 Bring the stock to a simmer in a large frying pan or shallow casserole covered with a lid. Add the pearl barley, cover and cook for 10 mins. Then add the potatoes and cook, covered, for 12–15 mins until tender.

2 Remove the lid, increase the heat and bubble the stock for a few mins to reduce. Stir in the greens, crème fraîche, dill, zest and juice. If you're freezing, cool at this stage. If eating straight away, simmer for 3–4 mins until veg is just tender.

3 Just before serving, stir in the prawns to heat through and season to taste. If freezing, cool completely then scatter the prawns on top and freeze. Defrost fully in the fridge overnight then gently bring back to a simmer, uncovered, until veg is tender and prawns hot through.

Nutrition per serving
kcal 233 • fat 2g • saturates none • carbs 31g • sugars 4g • fibre 4g • protein 24g • salt 1.43g

Sweet & sour chicken & veg

A trusty takeaway favourite just got superhealthy. Make ahead and freeze for Friday!

EASY ⏱ PREP 20 mins COOK 20 mins ⏳ SERVES 4

- 425g can pineapple chunks, drained, juice reserved
- 2 tbsp each tomato ketchup, malt vinegar and cornflour
- 1 tbsp vegetable oil
- 1 onion, chopped
- 1 red chilli, deseeded and sliced
- 1 red and green pepper, chopped
- 2 carrots, sliced on the diagonal
- 2 skinless chicken breasts, thinly sliced
- 125g pack baby corn, sliced lengthways
- 2 tomatoes, quartered
- cooked rice, to serve

1 Make the sweet & sour sauce by whisking together the pineapple juice, tomato ketchup, malt vinegar and cornflour. There should be 300ml – add water or stock if you're short.

2 Heat the oil in a frying pan or wok over a high heat. Add the onion, chilli, peppers, carrots and chicken and stir-fry for 3–5 mins until the vegetables are starting to soften and the chicken is almost cooked.

3 Add the corn and sauce. Bubble for 2 mins, add the tomatoes and cook for 2 mins until the sauce thickens, the chicken is cooked and the vegetables are tender. Freeze at this point if you like, or eat straight away with rice.

Nutrition per serving
kcal 230 • fat 4g • saturates 1g • carbs 30g • sugar 24g • protein 20g • fibre 4g • salt 0.26g

Red lentil & carrot soup

This warming and budget-friendly vegetarian soup is perfect packed in a flask for lunch. It's also easy to double the quantities and freeze half for later.

EASY ⏱ PREP 5 mins COOK 20 mins ◷ SERVES 2

- 1 medium-large onion
- 2 tsp olive oil
- 3 garlic cloves
- 2 carrots, scrubbed
- 85g red lentils
- 1 vegetable stock cube, crumbled
- parsley sprigs, chopped (about 2 tbsp), plus a few extra leaves

1. Boil the kettle while you finely slice the onion. Heat the oil in a medium pan, add the onion and fry for 2 mins. Meanwhile, slice the garlic and dice the carrots. Add them to the pan, and cook briefly.
2. Pour in 1 litre of the boiling water, stir in the lentils and stock cube, then cover the pan and cook over a medium heat for 15 mins until the lentils are tender. Take off the heat and cool and freeze in freezer bags or containers to serve later or stir in the parsley, then ladle into bowls and scatter with extra parsley leaves, if you like.

Nutrition per serving
kcal 258 • fat 5g • saturates 1g • carbs 37g • sugars 12g • fibre 8g • protein 13g • salt 1.6g

Beetroot & onion seed soup

A deep red autumnal soup that's low fat, vegetarian and full of flavour. Beetroot and apple give this soup a subtle sweet flavour, while lentils add protein and bulk.

EASY ⏱ PREP 5 mins COOK 5 mins ⏲ SERVES 1

- 250g cooked beetroot
- 100g canned lentils
- 1 small apple
- 1 crushed garlic clove
- 1 tsp onion seeds (nigella), plus extra to serve
- 250ml vegetable stock

1 Tip the beetroot, lentils, apple, garlic and onion seeds into a blender with the vegetable stock and some seasoning, and blitz until smooth. *Freeze at this point if you like.* Heat until piping hot in the microwave or on the hob, then scatter over some extra onion seeds, if you like.

Nutrition per serving
kcal 257 • fat 2g • saturates none • carbs 41g • sugars 30g • fibre 10g • protein 12g • salt 1.2g

Sweetcorn & smoked haddock chowder

Keep smoked haddock fillets and sweetcorn in the freezer, and add a few storecupboard staples for this tasty chowder.

MORE EFFORT ⏱ PREP 10 mins COOK 20 mins ◷ SERVES 2

- knob of butter
- 2 rashers streaky bacon, chopped
- 1 onion, finely chopped
- 500ml milk
- 350g potatoes (about 2 medium), cut into small cubes
- 300g frozen smoked haddock fillets (about 2)
- 140g frozen sweetcorn
- chopped parsley, to serve (optional)

1 Heat the butter in a large saucepan. Tip in the bacon, then cook until starting to brown. Add the onion, cook until soft, then pour over the milk and stir through the potatoes. Bring to the boil, then simmer for 5 mins.

2 Add the haddock, then leave to gently cook for another 10 mins. By now the fish should have defrosted so you can break it into large chunks. Stir through the sweetcorn, then cook for another few mins until the fish is cooked through and the sweetcorn has defrosted. Cool and freeze in freezer bags or containers. To eat, scatter over parsley, if using. Serve with plenty of crusty bread.

Nutrition per serving
kcal 550 • fat 16g • saturates 7g • sugars 18g • carbs 59g • fibre 4g • protein 47g • salt 3.92g

Creamy leek & bean soup

This healthy, low-fat soup is based on the classic leek and potato, but cannellini beans replace the potatoes – as they contribute to your 5-a-day.

EASY · PREP 10 mins COOK 20 mins · SERVES 4

- 1 tbsp rapeseed oil
- 600g leeks, well washed and thinly sliced
- 1 litre hot vegetable bouillon
- 2 x 400g cans cannellini beans, drained
- 2 large garlic cloves, finely grated
- 100g baby spinach
- 150ml full-fat milk

1 Heat the oil in a large pan, add the leeks and cook on a low-medium heat for 5 mins. Pour in the bouillon, tip in the beans, cover and simmer for 10 mins.
2 Stir in the garlic and spinach, cover the pan and cook for 5 mins more until the spinach has wilted but still retains its fresh green colour.
3 Add the milk and plenty of black pepper, and blitz with a stick blender until smooth. Ladle into bowls. Chill or freeze the remainder.

Nutrition per serving
kcal 218 · fat 6g · saturates 1g · carbs 26g · sugars 7g · fibre 6g · protein 12g · salt 0.9g

Pumpkin & bacon soup

The soft, sweet flesh of the Crown Prince pumpkin is perfect for this silky soup. Butternut or onion squash are good alternatives.

EASY   PREP 10 mins COOK 1 hr 10 mins   SERVES 4

- 1 tbsp vegetable oil
- 50g butter
- 1 onion, finely chopped
- 150g maple-cured bacon, cut into small pieces
- ½ Crown Prince pumpkin or onion squash, peeled, deseeded and cut into medium chunks (you need about 500g pumpkin flesh)
- 1 litre chicken stock
- 100ml double cream
- 3 tbsp pumpkin seeds, toasted
- maple syrup, for drizzling

1 In a large, heavy-bottomed pan, heat the oil with 25g butter. Add the onion and a pinch of salt and cook on a low heat for 10 mins or until soft. Add 60g bacon and cook for a further 5 mins until the bacon releases its fat. Then increase the heat to medium, add the pumpkin and stock and season. Bring to the boil, then reduce the heat to a simmer, cover with a lid and cook for about 40 mins until the pumpkin is soft.

2 Pour in the cream, bring to the boil again and remove from the heat. Set aside some of the liquid, then blend the remaining pumpkin until smooth and velvety, adding liquid back into the pan bit by bit as you go (add more liquid if you like it thinner). Strain through a fine sieve, check the seasoning and set aside. Freeze the soup at this point and finish it once defrosted.

3 Melt the remaining butter in a pan over a high heat and fry the rest of the bacon with black pepper for 5 mins. Divide the bacon among four bowls, reheat the soup and pour over. To serve, sprinkle over the pumpkin seeds and drizzle with maple syrup.

Nutrition per serving
kcal 557 • fat 43g • saturates 20g • carbs 19g • sugars 12g • fibre 5g • protein 21g • salt 2.2g

Hot 'n' spicy roasted red pepper & tomato soup

Whizz up this warming and vibrant soup in 10 minutes for a filling veggie supper, rich in vitamin C.

EASY ⏱ PREP 5 mins COOK 5 mins 🕐 SERVES 1

- 290g roasted red peppers, drained
- 270g cherry tomatoes, halved
- 1 garlic clove, crushed
- 1 vegetable stock cube
- 1 tsp paprika
- 1 tbsp olive oil
- 4 tbsp ground almonds

1 Put the roasted red peppers in a blender with the cherry tomatoes, garlic, vegetable stock cube, 100ml water, paprika, olive oil and ground almonds. Blitz until smooth, season well and heat until piping hot before serving. This will freeze well; you may need to add a little water or stock when you defrost it.

Nutrition per serving
kcal 631 • fat 48g • saturates 5g • carbs 23g • sugars 12g • fibre 5g • protein 23g • salt 3.0g

Carrot & ginger soup

Give yourself a boost and treat yourself to this low-fat, healthy carrot soup with a swirl of soured cream.

EASY ⏱ PREP 5 mins COOK 5 mins 🕒 SERVES 1

- 3 large carrots
- 1 tbsp grated ginger
- 1 tsp turmeric
- a pinch of cayenne pepper, plus extra to serve
- 20g wholemeal bread
- 1 tbsp soured cream, plus extra to serve
- 200ml vegetable stock

1 Peel and chop the carrots and put in a blender with the ginger, turmeric, cayenne pepper, wholemeal bread, soured cream and vegetable stock. Blitz until smooth. Chill and freeze the soup at this point if you like.

2 Heat until piping hot. Swirl through some extra soured cream, or a sprinkling of cayenne, if you like.

Nutrition per serving
kcal 223 • fat 7g • saturates 3g • carbs 30g • sugars 19g • fibre 10g • protein 5g • salt 1.1g

Spinach & watercress soup

Go veggie, go green and go filling! This simple and vibrant soup is healthy, 3 of your 5-a-day and ready in 10 minutes.

EASY 🕐 PREP 5 mins COOK 5 mins 🕐 SERVES 1

- 100g spinach
- 100g watercress
- 1 spring onion, sliced
- 100ml vegetable stock
- ½ an avocado
- 100g cooked rice
- juice ½ lemon
- 2 tbsp mixed seeds, plus extra to serve

1 Put the spinach, watercress, spring onion, vegetable stock, avocado, cooked rice, lemon juice and mixed seeds in a blender with seasoning. Whizz until smooth. Freeze the soup at this point if you like.
2 To serve, heat until piping hot. Scatter over some toasted seeds if you want added crunch.

Nutrition per serving
kcal 457 • fat 26g • saturates 5g • carbs 33g • sugars 2g • fibre 9g • protein 18g • salt 0.5g

Moroccan harira

This is a healthy vegetarian version of the classic Moroccan soup with plenty of cumin, turmeric and cinnamon, each offering different health benefits, plus it's low in fat and calories too.

EASY · PREP 15 mins COOK 40 mins · SERVES 4

- 1–2 tbsp rapeseed oil
- 2 large onions, finely chopped
- 4 garlic cloves, chopped
- 2 tsp turmeric
- 2 tsp cumin
- ½ tsp cinnamon
- 2 red chillies, deseeded and sliced
- 500g carton passata
- 1.7 litres reduced-salt vegetable bouillon
- 175g dried green lentils
- 2 carrots, chopped into pieces
- 1 sweet potato, peeled and diced
- 5 celery sticks, chopped into small pieces
- ⅔ small pack coriander, few sprigs reserved, the rest chopped
- 1 lemon, cut into 4 wedges, to serve

1 Heat the oil in a large non-stick sauté pan over a medium heat and fry the onions and garlic until starting to soften. Tip in the spices and chilli, stir briefly, then pour in the passata and stock. Add the lentils, carrots, sweet potato and celery, and bring to the boil.

2 Cover the pan and leave to simmer for 30 mins, then cook uncovered for a further 5–10 mins until the vegetables and lentils are tender. Freeze the soup now if you don't want to eat it straight away. Stir in the chopped coriander and serve in bowls with lemon wedges for squeezing over, and the reserved coriander sprinkled over.

Nutrition per serving
kcal 335 • fat 6g • saturates 1g • carbs 48g • sugars 21g • fibre 13g • protein 16g • salt 0.2g

Summer carrot, tarragon & white bean soup

This satisfying, low-fat, low-calorie vegan soup provides 3 of your 5-a-day. It's suitable for freezing, so why not make a few meals out of it?

EASY ⏱ PREP 10 mins COOK 20 mins ◔ SERVES 4

- 1 tbsp rapeseed oil
- 2 large leeks, well washed, halved lengthways and finely sliced
- 700g carrots, chopped
- 1.4 litres hot reduced-salt vegetable bouillon (we used Marigold)
- 4 garlic cloves, finely grated
- 2 x 400g cans cannellini beans in water
- $^2/_3$ small pack tarragon, leaves roughly chopped

1 Heat the oil over a medium heat in a large pan and fry the leeks and carrots for 5 mins to soften.
2 Pour over the stock, stir in the garlic, the beans with their liquid, and three-quarters of the tarragon, then cover and simmer for 15 mins or until the veg is just tender. Freeze at this point. Stir in the remaining tarragon before serving.

Nutrition per serving
kcal 271 • fat 6g • saturates 1g • carbs 38g • sugars 17g • fibre 13g • protein 11g • salt 0.7g

Supergreen soup with yogurt & pine nuts

A simple low-fat soup that's a fresh new way to use a bag of mixed leaves – it's rich in vitamin C, fibre, folate and calcium too.

EASY 🕐 PREP 5 mins COOK 25 mins 🕒 SERVES 2

- 2 tsp olive oil
- 1 onion, chopped
- 2 garlic cloves, crushed
- 1 potato (approx 250g), cut into small cubes
- 600ml vegetable stock
- 120g bag mixed watercress, rocket and spinach salad
- 150g pot natural yogurt
- 20g pine nuts, toasted
- chilli oil, to serve (optional)

1 Heat the oil in a medium saucepan over a low-medium heat. Add the onion and a pinch of salt, then cook slowly, stirring occasionally, for 10 mins until softened but not coloured. Add the garlic and cook for 1 min more.

2 Tip in the potato followed by the veg stock. Simmer for 10–12 mins until the potato is soft enough that a cutlery knife will slide in easily. Add the bag of salad and let it wilt for 1 min, then blitz the soup in a blender until it's completely smooth. Freeze the soup at this point.

3 Serve with a dollop of yogurt, some toasted pine nuts and a drizzle of chilli oil, if you like.

Nutrition per serving
kcal 325 • fat 13g • saturates 2g • carbs 36g • sugars 14g • fibre 7g • protein 12g • salt 1.0g

Turkey minestrone

A warm and comforting turkey soup recipe to put your Christmas leftovers to good use, or used bought cooked turkey at any time of year.

EASY ⏱ PREP 15 mins COOK 40 mins ◔ SERVES 6

- 2 tsp olive oil
- 100g smoked bacon lardons
- 1 red onion, finely chopped
- 1 carrot, finely chopped
- 1 celery stick, finely chopped
- 2 garlic cloves, finely chopped
- 2 bay leaves
- 2 thyme sprigs
- 300g celeriac (or any other root veg), cut into cubes
- 200g potato, cut into cubes
- 400g can borlotti beans, drained and rinsed
- 1.5 litres turkey or chicken stock (fresh is best)
- 350g cooked turkey
- 100g orzo
- 75g curly kale, shredded

1 Heat 1 tsp of oil in a large saucepan. Add the bacon and fry over a medium-to-high heat for 4–5 mins or until golden, then set aside.
2 Put the remaining oil, the onion, carrot, celery and a pinch of salt in the pan. Cook gently over a low heat for 8–10 mins, stirring occasionally, until the veg is soft but not coloured. Add the garlic and herbs, and cook for 2 mins more.
3 Tip in the celeriac, potato, borlotti beans and turkey or chicken stock. Bring to the boil, then simmer, uncovered, for 10–15 mins. Add the cooked turkey, orzo and the bacon, and cook for 10 mins. Freeze at this point and then add the kale when you have defrosted the soup.
4 Just before serving, tip in the kale, give everything a good stir and return to the heat for about 2 mins or until the kale has wilted.

Nutrition per serving
kcal 345 • fat 8g • saturates 3g • carbs 28g • sugars 4g • fibre 8g • protein 36g • salt 1.5g

Creamy artichoke soup with Parmesan skins

Artichoke makes this soup ultra silky and the crispy skins add a hit of crunch and flavour – perfect as a starter for dinner with friends.

EASY ⏱ PREP 30 mins COOK 25 mins 🕒 SERVES 4

- juice ½ lemon
- 500g Jerusalem artichokes
- 2 tsp vegetable oil
- 25g butter
- 1 onion, roughly chopped
- 1 floury potato (about 140g), such as King Edward, roughly chopped
- 600ml vegetable or chicken stock
- 3 tbsp whipping or double cream, plus a little extra to serve (optional)
- 1–2 tbsp finely grated Parmesan or vegetarian cheese
- 1 rosemary sprig, leaves only, finely chopped

1 Half-fill a large bowl with water and add the lemon juice. Peel the artichokes, then toss the peelings with the vegetable oil in a bowl and set aside. Chop the artichokes into rough chunks and submerge them in the lemony water.
2 Melt the butter in a large saucepan, and add the onion, potato and seasoning. Drain the artichokes and stir them in. Cover the pan and sweat gently for 15 mins, stirring now and again.
3 Pour in the stock, cover and simmer for 10–15 mins until the vegetables are completely tender. Whizz the soup in a blender or with a stick blender until very smooth, return to the pan, then add the cream and season to taste.
4 Meanwhile, prepare the skins. Heat oven to 220C/200C fan/gas 7 and line a baking sheet with baking parchment (not foil, they will stick). Scatter the skins over, and roast for 10 mins. Turn them over, scatter with the Parmesan and rosemary and roast for 5 mins more or until crisp and dry, then season with a pinch of flaky salt and pepper. Freeze the soup and skins separately if you are making them ahead and re-crisp the skins before serving. Serve the soup in bowls, add a swirl more cream (if you like) and top with the crisp skins.

Nutrition per serving
kcal 371 • fat 21g • saturates 12g • carbs 31g • sugars 15g • fibre 4g • protein 11g • salt 0.7g

Neeps & tatties soup

Enjoy a taste of Scotland in our warming soup with swede, potato and haggis topping. It's Burns Night in a bowl.

EASY ⏱ PREP 15 mins COOK 35 mins ⏳ SERVES 2 FOR LUNCH OR 4 AS A STARTER

- 25g butter
- ¼ tsp ground coriander
- 1 onion, chopped
- ½ medium-sized swede (about 200g), peeled and chopped into small pieces
- 1 carrot, sliced
- 1 celery stick, sliced into small pieces
- 140g potatoes, chopped into small pieces
- good grating of nutmeg
- 400ml milk
- 140g cooked haggis or black pudding, chopped or crumbled into pieces
- 2 tbsp double cream
- a few celery leaves, torn

1 Melt the butter in a large saucepan over a medium heat. Add the coriander and the vegetables, fry for 4–5 mins, then cover with 400ml water and bring to the boil. Cook until all the vegetables are soft – around 20–25 mins.

2 Season with salt, pepper and nutmeg, then add the milk. Transfer to a blender or blitz with a stick blender until smooth, then return to the pan to heat through. (For a really smooth consistency, push the mixture through a sieve after blending.) Check the seasoning and add a little more salt and nutmeg, if you like. Freeze the soup at this point if you like and finish the garnish when you defrost it.

3 To serve, heat the cooked haggis or black pudding in a frying pan until sizzling. Serve the soup in bowls and top with the haggis or black pudding, a swirl of double cream and the celery leaves.

Nutrition per serving (4)
kcal 260 • fat 15g • saturates 7g • carbs 22g • sugars 9g • fibre 3g • protein 9g • salt 1.0g

Chunky vegetable & brown rice soup

Brown rice makes this vitamin-packed soup a great low-GI option. If you like, serve it puréed for a change.

EASY PREP 20 mins COOK 50 mins SERVES 4

- 2 tbsp cold-pressed rapeseed oil
- 1 medium onion, halved and sliced
- 2 garlic cloves, finely sliced
- 2 celery sticks, trimmed and thinly sliced
- 2 medium carrots, cut into chunks
- 2 medium parsnips, cut into chunks
- 1 tbsp finely chopped thyme leaves
- 100g wholegrain rice
- 2 medium leeks, sliced.
- small pack parsley, to garnish

1 Heat the oil in a large non-stick pan and add the onion, garlic, celery, carrots, parsnips and thyme. Cover with a lid and cook gently for 15 mins, stirring occasionally, until the onions are softened and beginning to colour. Add the rice and pour in 1.2 litres cold water. Bring to the boil. Reduce the heat to a simmer and cook, uncovered, for 15 mins, stirring occasionally.

2 Season the soup with plenty of ground black pepper and salt to taste, then stir in the leeks. Return to a gentle simmer and cook for a further 5 mins or until the leeks have softened. Adjust the seasoning to taste and blitz half the soup with a stick blender, leaving the other half chunky, if you like. Top with the parsley and serve in deep bowls. This will freeze for up to 3 weeks if you want to make it ahead.

Nutrition per serving
kcal 261 • fat 8g • saturates 1g • carbs 37g • sugars 11g • fibre 10g • protein 5g • salt 0.5g

Carrot & coriander soup

Everyone loves this super healthy soup, perfect for an easy supper.

EASY ⏱ PREP 15 mins COOK 30 mins ◔ SERVES 4

- 1 tbsp vegetable oil
- 1 onion, chopped
- 1 tsp ground coriander
- 1 potato, chopped
- 450g carrots, peeled and chopped
- 1.2 litres vegetable or chicken stock
- handful coriander (about ½ a supermarket packet)

1 Heat the oil in a large pan, add the onion, then fry for 5 mins until softened. Stir in the ground coriander and potato, then cook for 1 min. Add the carrots and stock, bring to the boil, then reduce the heat. Cover and cook for 20 mins until the carrots are tender.

2 Tip into a food processor with the coriander, then blitz until smooth (you may need to do this in 2 batches). Return to pan, taste, add salt if necessary. If freezing, cool and portion into freezerproof containers. Reheat to serve.

Nutrition per serving
kcal 115 • 4g fat • 1g saturates • 19g carbs • 12g sugars • 5g fibre • 3g protein • 0.46g salt

Red lentil & coconut soup

This light vegetarian soup is enriched with creamy coconut milk and packed with nutritious ingredients like ginger, spinach and limes.

EASY ⏱ PREP 5 mins COOK 30 mins ⏱ SERVES 4

- 100g red lentils
- 1 heaped tsp turmeric
- 1 tbsp coarsely grated ginger
- 2 garlic cloves, sliced
- 1 litre vegetable stock
- 400ml can coconut milk
- 2 leeks, well washed and sliced
- 2 handfuls baby spinach (approx 50g)
- 2 limes, cut into wedges

1 Tip the lentils into a large pan and add the turmeric, ginger and garlic. Pour in the stock, then cover the pan and simmer for 15 mins until the lentils have softened.
2 Pour in the coconut milk, stir in the leeks, cover and cook for 10 mins more.
3 Add the spinach and cook just to wilt it, then spoon into bowls and squeeze over the lime juice. Freeze before adding the lime and then add it when you have reheated the soup.

Nutrition per serving
kcal 314 • fat 19g • saturates 15g • carbs 22g • sugars 6g • fibre 6g • protein 10g • salt 0.7g

Carrot & ginger soup

Low-fat and warming, this bean and vegetable soup makes a healthy lunch or dinner – for even more nutrients, top with sliced almonds.

EASY ⏱ PREP 15 mins COOK 30 mins 🍽 SERVES 4

- 1 tbsp rapeseed oil
- 1 large onion, chopped
- 2 tbsp coarsely grated ginger
- 2 garlic cloves, sliced
- ½ tsp ground nutmeg
- 850ml vegetable stock
- 500g carrots (preferably organic), sliced
- 400g can cannellini beans (no need to drain)

FOR THE TOPPING
- 4 tbsp almonds in their skins, cut into slivers
- sprinkle of nutmeg

1 Heat the oil in a large pan, add the onion, ginger and garlic, and fry for 5 mins until starting to soften. Stir in the nutmeg and cook for 1 min more.
2 Pour in the stock, add the carrots, beans and their liquid, then cover and simmer for 20–25 mins until the carrots are tender.
3 Scoop a third of the mixture into a bowl and blitz the remainder with a hand blender or in a food processor until smooth. Freeze now if you like. Return everything to the pan and heat until bubbling. Serve topped with the almonds and nutmeg.

Nutrition per serving
kcal 293 • fat 12g • saturates 1g • carbs 31g • sugars 19g • fibre 8g • protein 10g • salt 0.9g

Bone broth

This nutritious soup, made from chicken bones and flavoured with bay, lemon and herbs, is packed with nutrients for healthy bones, hair and nails.

A LITTLE EFFORT ⏱ PREP 20 mins COOK 45 mins ⬤ SERVES 4

- 1 meaty chicken carcass, plus any jellified roasting juices from it, skin and fat discarded
- 1 large onion, halved and sliced
- zest and juice 1 lemon
- 2 bay leaves
- 1–2 red chillies, halved, deseeded and sliced
- 1 tsp ground coriander
- ½ tsp ground cumin
- small pack coriander, stems and leaves chopped and separated
- 1 large garlic clove, finely grated

FOR THE TOPPING
- 250g pouch wholegrain basmati rice

1 Break the chicken carcass into a large pan and add the onion, 1½ litres of water, the lemon juice and bay leaves. Cover and simmer for 40 mins. Remove from the heat and allow to cool slightly, to make things a bit easier to handle.

2 Place a colander over a bowl and scoop out all the bones into the colander. Pick through them, stripping off the chicken and returning it with any onion as you work your way down the pile of bones.

3 Return any broth from the bowl to the pan – and any jellified roasting juices – along with the chilli, ground coriander, cumin, coriander stems, lemon zest and garlic. Cook for a few mins until just bubbling – don't overboil as you will spoil the delicate flavours. Taste, and season only if you need to. Can be frozen at this point for up to 3 months. To serve, heat the rice following pack instructions, then toss with the coriander leaves. Ladle the broth into bowls and top with the rice.

Nutrition per serving
kcal 150 • fat 3g • saturates 1g • carbs 24g • sugars 5g • fibre 2g • protein 6g • salt 0.9g

Roasted sweet potato & carrot soup

This silky smooth, super versatile vegetarian soup is perfect for a dinner party starter, everyday dinner or warming lunch – with 2 of your 5-a-day.

EASY 🕐 PREP 15 mins COOK 35 mins 🕐 SERVES 4

- 500g sweet potatoes, peeled and cut into chunks
- 300g carrots, peeled and cut into chunks
- 3 tbsp olive oil
- 2 onions, finely chopped
- 2 garlic cloves, crushed
- 1 litre vegetable stock
- 100ml crème fraîche, plus extra to serve

1 Heat oven to 220C/200C fan/gas 7 and put the sweet potatoes and carrots into a large roasting tin, drizzled with 2 tbsp olive oil and plenty of seasoning. Roast the veg in the oven for 25–30 mins or until caramelised and tender.

2 Meanwhile, put the remaining 1 tbsp olive oil in a large deep saucepan and fry the onion over a medium-low heat for about 10 mins until softened. Add the garlic and stir for 1 min before adding the stock. Simmer for 5–10 mins until the onions are very soft, then set aside.

3 Once the roasted veg is done, leave to cool a little, then transfer to the saucepan and use a hand blender to process until smooth. Stir in the crème fraîche and a little more seasoning and reheat until hot or freeze for up to 3 months. Serve in soup bowls topped with a swirl of crème fraîche and a good grinding of black pepper.

Nutrition per serving
kcal 419 • fat 19g • saturates 8g • carbs 45g • sugars 27g • fibre 10g • protein 11g • salt 0.9g

Chilled pea soup with frozen mint & malt vinegar

Serve this silky smooth soup with flavoured ice cubes to keep it chilled – garnish with fresh peas and crispy bacon for a dinner party.

EASY 🕐 PREP 25 mins plus chilling and freezing COOK 25 mins 🕐 SERVES 6

- 75g butter
- 4 rashers smoked streaky bacon
- 1 onion, sliced
- 50g golden caster sugar
- 700g frozen peas, defrosted
- 10 mint leaves

FOR THE ICE CUBES
- 75ml distilled malt vinegar
- 4 tbsp demerara sugar
- ½ small bunch mint, leaves picked

TO SERVE
- 50g shelled fresh peas
- 50ml rapeseed oil
- a few small mint leaves

1 First, make the ice cubes. Bring 75ml water, the malt vinegar and sugar to the boil. Add the mint leaves and set aside to steep for 10 mins. Strain into a jug, then pour into 12 holes of an ice cube tray and freeze until solid.

2 In a heavy-based saucepan, heat the butter until foaming, add the bacon and fry until crispy. Remove using a slotted spoon and set aside. Add the onion to the pan and cook until soft, about 10 mins. Add the sugar and 400ml water, bring to the boil, then add the frozen peas and mint. Bring back to the boil for 1 min, then remove from the heat and leave to cool a little. Pour the soup into a blender and blend until smooth. Pass through a fine sieve into a bowl Taste and season. Cover with cling film and chill or freeze for up to 3 months until ready to serve.

3 Chop the crispy bacon into small bits. To serve, mix the bacon with the fresh peas and rapeseed oil in a bowl. Ladle the soup into your dishes and add the ice cubes (if you like, you can crush them bit too). Top with the bacon and peas, and scatter over a few mint leaves.

Nutrition per serving
kcal 423 • fat 23g • saturates 8g • carbs 37g • sugars 27g • fibre 10g • protein 11g • salt 0.6g

Creamy spring soup with goat's cheese & prosciutto toasts

Asparagus, peas and watercress blend beautifully in this vibrant green soup with ciabatta toasts – serve as a starter or a light lunch.

EASY ⏱ PREP 25 mins COOK 30 mins 🕐 SERVES 8

- 2 tbsp olive or rapeseed oil
- 1 onion, chopped
- 1 fennel bulb, chopped
- 200g asparagus, woody ends and all, roughly chopped (save the pretty tips for another recipe, if you like)
- 2 garlic cloves, crushed
- 1 tsp fennel seeds
- 1.2 litres vegetable stock
- 450g frozen peas
- 100g bag watercress, reserve some small leaves for the toasts
- small bunch parsley, roughly chopped
- small bunch mint, leaves picked and roughly chopped (or buy 1 large bunch and use half in the pesto, if making)
- 100ml double cream

FOR THE TOASTS
- 1 large ciabatta, thickly sliced on an angle
- drizzle of extra virgin olive or rapeseed oil, plus extra for serving
- 1 fat garlic clove, squashed
- 150g pack soft goat's cheese
- 6 slices prosciutto
- 200g pesto

1 Heat the oil in a large pan. Add the onion and fennel and fry gently for 10 mins or until softened but not coloured. Add the asparagus, garlic and fennel seeds and stir everything around in the pan for another 1–2 mins. Pour in the vegetable stock, season, and cover with a lid. Leave on a gentle simmer for no longer than 5 mins. Cool and freeze at this point.

2 To serve heat the grill. Put the ciabatta slices on a baking tray and drizzle with a little oil. Pop the bread under the grill for 2–3 mins each side or until golden and crisp. Remove the toasts and rub the garlic over each piece of toast.

3 Defrost the soup and bring it back to a simmer, add the peas to the soup, bubble for 1 min to defrost the peas, then remove the pan from the heat and add most of the watercress, the herbs and the double cream. Use a hand blender to blitz it to a smooth, creamy consistency. Check the seasoning – you will need to be quite generous.

4 Spread each piece of toast with a little goat's cheese, then top with a slice of ruffled prosciutto, a dollop of pesto and a few small sprigs of watercress. Finally, drizzle over a little olive oil. Serve the toasts alongside the soup, with a bowl of pesto on the side.

Nutrition per serving
kcal 472 • fat 30g • saturates 10g • carbs 27g • sugars 6g • fibre 8g • protein 20g • salt 1.9g

The ultimate makeover burgers

Turn a barbecue favourite into a superhealthy treat without compromising on taste.

EASY ⏱ PREP 25 mins plus chilling COOK 45 mins ⏱ SERVES 4

FOR THE BURGERS
- 400g lean beef mince (10% fat), preferably organic
- 5 spring onions, finely chopped
- 140g finely grated carrot
- 2 garlic cloves, finely chopped
- 2 tsp Dijon mustard
- 1 tbsp chopped tarragon
- 1 medium egg, beaten
- 4 wholemeal bread rolls, split in half
- 1½ tsp rapeseed oil, for brushing
- 25g watercress

FOR THE ROASTED PEPPER SALSA
- 2 large red peppers halved lengthways and deseeded
- 100g cherry or baby plum tomatoes, halved
- 2 tsp lime juice
- 2 tsp snipped chives
- ¼ very small red onion, thinly sliced
- pinch crushed chillies

1 Tip the mince into a bowl with the spring onions, carrot, garlic, mustard, tarragon and egg. Mix well using a fork. Season with pepper and salt, then divide the mixture into 4. Flatten each piece into a 10cm round about 2cm thick – a similar width to the buns. Chill for 30 mins. The burgers can be made ahead: stack between pieces of greaseproof paper to stop them sticking, wrap in cling film, then chill or freeze until ready to cook.

2 Meanwhile, heat oven to 200C/fan 180C/gas 6. Lay the peppers, cut sides down, on a non-stick baking sheet. Roast for 35 mins until the skins are charred, laying the tomatoes next to them, cut-side up, for the final 3 mins just to soften slightly. Remove and immediately transfer the peppers to a small bowl and cover with cling film. Leave for 5–10 mins until cool enough to handle. Peel off the pepper skins, chop the peppers and tip them back into the bowl to join any juices there. Chop the tomatoes and stir into the peppers with the lime juice, chives, onion and chillies. Taste and add a grind of pepper if needed. Set aside. Can be made 1–2 days ahead and chilled.

3 Heat a griddle pan, or cook the burgers on the barbecue. Lay the cut sides of the buns on the griddle and cook until marked with the griddle bars. Brush each burger on one side with some of the rapeseed oil. Place on the hot griddle, oiled side down. Cook – don't move them or they may stick – for 5 mins for medium, brush the unoiled side with the rest of the oil, then turn and cook for another 5 mins. (For well done, add an extra 1–2 mins to each side.)

4 Remove and let the burgers rest for 2–3 mins. Drizzle a little of the pepper juices over the bottom of each bun to moisten, lay on some watercress sprigs, top with a burger, then a spoonful of the salsa, spooning over some more of the juices. Sandwich together with the tops of the buns.

Nutrition per serving
kcal 405 • fat 15.4g • saturates 5g • carbs 37g • sugars 10g • fibre 5g • protein 32g • salt 1.44g

Classic chunky fish cakes

Fish cakes are a great freezer staple as they are ready portioned so you can defrost as many as you need.

EASY · PREP 40 mins COOK 30 mins · MAKES 12

- 1kg potatoes, peeled and chopped
- 1kg mix salmon and coley fillets
- zest and juice 1 lemon
- bunch each dill, chives, parsley and spring onions, chopped
- 4 tbsp tartar sauce, plus extra to serve if you like
- 3 eggs, beaten
- 100g plain flour
- 250g breadcrumbs
- 2 tbsp olive oil

1 Cover the potatoes in cold, salted water and bring to the boil. Turn down to a simmer and cook for 10–12 mins until tender. Drain and steam dry for a few mins, then mash and set aside to cool a little. Meanwhile, cook the fish. Cover in cold water and the lemon juice, bring to a gentle simmer, then poach for 5 mins (depending on the thickness of the fish) until just cooked through. Remove from the water, get rid of the skin and flake into large chunks.

2 Put the lemon zest, herbs, spring onions, tartar sauce and some seasoning into a large bowl with the fish and the potatoes. Combine all the ingredients, then divide into 12 and shape into cakes.

3 Put the eggs, flour and breadcrumbs on 3 plates. Dip each of the fish cakes in flour, pat off any excess, then dip in the egg. Finally, coat in the breadcrumbs and transfer to a clean plate or baking tray lined with parchment paper. Repeat with the remaining fish cakes. You can freeze the fish cakes now, or chill for 1–2 days.

4 To cook, heat the grill to medium. Brush the fish cakes with the oil and grill for 4–5 mins each side until golden and hot through. Serve with extra tartar sauce and salad or green veg. Defrost frozen fish cakes overnight in the fridge and cook as above, or cook straight from frozen, giving them more time.

Nutrition per fish cake
kcal 330 • fat 10g • saturates 2g • carbs 38g • sugar 2g • fibre 2g • protein 23g • salt 0.71g

Prawn & cod cakes

Make the most of leftover mash with these superhealthy fishcakes.

EASY ⏱ PREP 30 mins plus chilling COOK 35 mins ◔ SERVES 4

- 250g cod loin, skinless and boneless
- 175g cooked king prawns, chopped
- 175g mashed potato
- small bunch chives, snipped
- zest 1 lemon, plus 1 lemon cut into wedges, to serve
- 5 eggs, 1 beaten
- 50g breadcrumbs
- 2 tsp olive oil
- 200g green beans
- 100g cherry tomatoes
- 1 tbsp white wine vinegar

1 Heat the oven to 220C/200C fan/gas 7. In a small saucepan, cover the cod with cold water and gently poach for 3–4 mins until just cooked through. Remove with a slotted spoon and pat dry. Flake into a medium bowl with the prawns, potato and most of the chives, lemon zest and some seasoning. Shape into 4 even-size cakes and chill for 10 mins. Can be frozen: separate each one with a piece of parchment first.

2 Dip each cake in the beaten egg, then coat in the breadcrumbs, repeat with the remaining fish cakes. Brush each cake with 1 tsp of the olive oil, place on a roasting tray and cook for 25 mins, turning halfway through. Cook beans in salted boiling water for 3–4 mins, until tender, adding the tomatoes for the final min. Drain and toss through the remaining oil, vinegar and reserved chives, mashing the tomatoes lightly with a fork, season with some black pepper and set aside.

3 For the poached eggs, bring a shallow pan of water to just boiling, stir the water once or twice and crack in the eggs. Poach for 3–4 mins, then remove with a slotted spoon. Serve the fishcakes topped with a poached egg and garnished with the beans and a few wedges of lemon for squeezing over.

Nutrition per serving
kcal 333 • fat 14g • saturates 3g • carbs 20g • sugars 4g • fibre 2g • protein 34g • salt 1.47g

Beef schnitzel

Cover minute steaks in a light breadcrumb coating and pan-fry until crisp and golden.

EASY ⊙ PREP 20 mins COOK 10 mins ⊕ SERVES 5

- 5 thin-cut minute steaks
- 50g plain flour
- 2 tsp paprika
- 2 eggs, lightly beaten
- 250g dried breadcrumbs
- 5 tsp butter
- 5 tsp olive oil
- lemon wedges, to serve

1 Stretch a piece of cling film over a chopping board, lay the steaks on top of it, then put another piece of cling film on top. Use a rolling pin to bash the steaks until they are really flat and thin.
2 Mix the flour and paprika with some salt and pepper on a plate. Put the egg and breadcrumbs on two more plates, then dip the steaks into the flour first, then the egg, then the breadcrumbs. Wrap and freeze at this point if you like.
3 Heat 1 tsp of butter and 1 tsp of oil in a large frying pan, then cook one of the schnitzels for about 1 min on each side. Repeat with the remaining schnitzels.

Nutrition per serving
kcal 468 • fat 14g • saturates 4g • carbs 46g • sugars 3g • fibre 2g • protein 43g • salt 0.82g

Bake-from-the-freezer pizzas

Load up these easy homemade pizza bases with your favourite toppings and freeze for a quick midweek dinner.

EASY 🕐 PREP 30 mins plus rising COOK 15 mins 🕐 MAKES 6

- 500g pack bread mix or pizza base mix
- little plain flour, for rolling
- 6 tbsp tomato pasta sauce or passata
- small bunch basil leaves, shredded
- 18 cherry tomatoes, halved
- 250g ball mozzarella, torn
- 25g Parmesan or vegetarian cheese, grated

1 Make up the bread dough following pack instructions, and transfer to an oiled bowl to rise for about 1 hr.
2 Knock back in the bowl by squashing all the air out of the dough with your fist. Divide the dough into 6 and roll each one on a lightly floured surface to a circle about 18cm in diameter. Put dough you're not using under a damp tea towel or oiled cling film to stop it drying out.
3 Put the pizza bases on large oiled baking sheets – you may need 2 or 3. Spread 1 tbsp sauce or passata on each base, then scatter on the basil, tomatoes, mozzarella and Parmesan (or whatever you fancy). You can freeze the pizzas now, if you like, on the baking sheets, wrapped in cling film. Or if eating straight away, heat the oven to 240C/220C fan/gas 9. Cook for 8–12 mins, until crisp and golden. To cook from frozen, remove the cling film and heat the oven to 220C/200C fan/gas 7. Bake for 10–14 mins until crisp and golden.

Nutrition per pizza
kcal 380 • fat 13g • saturates 7g • carbs 51g • sugar 4g • fibre 5g • protein 18g • salt 2.53g

Pea, pesto & sausage lasagne

Switch up your classic family lasagne with pesto, broccoli, mascarpone and chunks of sausage in a dish that's rich in calcium, folate, fibre and vitamin C.

EASY ⏲ PREP 10 mins COOK 55 mins ⏱ SERVES 4–6

- 4 tbsp olive oil
- 6 good-quality sausages, meat squeezed from the skins and rolled into cherry-tomato-sized balls
- small head of broccoli (about 400g), cut into small florets
- 250g (small punnet) cherry tomatoes, halved
- 200g frozen peas
- 400g mascarpone
- 150g tub fresh pesto
- large bunch basil, chopped
- 12 lasagne sheets
- 50ml milk
- 100g grated mozzarella
- 3 tbsp grated Parmesan
- 20g pine nuts

1 Heat half the oil in a large pan. Add the sausage balls and sizzle for 5–10 mins, rolling around until browned on all sides. Meanwhile, bring a pan of water to the boil, add the broccoli and cook for 3–4 mins until really tender. Drain well.

2 Heat the oven to 200C/180C fan/gas 6. Put the tomatoes on a baking tray, drizzle over the remaining oil, season well and roast for 10 mins until just softened. Stir the broccoli, peas, half the mascarpone, the pesto and basil into the sausage balls, simmer for a few mins until you have a nice sauce consistency, then check the seasoning.

3 Scoop a third of the mixture into a casserole dish, about 25 x 35cm, top with a third of the tomatoes, then arrange 3 lasagne sheets on top. Continue layering in the same way, reserving a few tomatoes and finishing with the pasta sheets.

4 Mix the milk into the remaining mascarpone to make a white sauce consistency. Pour this over the top of the pasta, then top with the mozzarella, Parmesan, pine nuts and the reserved tomatoes. Bake for 35–40 mins until golden brown and bubbling. If the lasagne is getting too dark, cover it with foil and continue cooking. Serve with a green salad. Can be cooled and frozen for up to 3 months; defrost thoroughly and reheat until piping hot in the centre.

Nutrition per serving (6)
kcal 844 • fat 71g • saturates 32g • carbs 33g • sugars 10g • fibre 7g • protein 25g • salt 1.6g

Slow-cooked Spanish chicken

Tangy olives, sweet peppers and spicy chorizo pack plenty of flavour into this dish. Serve it with rice or pasta, even crusty bread if you want to keep it really simple – you won't want to waste any of the delicious juices.

EASY ⏱ PREP 15 mins COOK 6 hrs 20 mins ⏲ SERVES 6

- 2 tbsp olive oil
- 1 Spanish onion, halved and sliced
- 12 large bone-in chicken thighs, skin removed
- 225g pack chorizo picante, thickly sliced
- pack of 3 mixed colour peppers, cut into chunks
- 150g (drained weight) pitted Spanish pimiento-stuffed green olives
- 300ml dry white wine (serve the rest of the bottle with the meal)
- 300ml chicken stock
- 1 tbsp tomato purée

1 Heat the oil in a large frying pan. Fry the onion for about 5 mins until golden. Tip into a slow cooker pot (we used a 6.5-litre model), then fry the chicken and chorizo in the same pan until starting to colour – you will need to do this in 2 batches. Add to the slow cooker with the peppers and olives.

2 Tip the wine, stock and tomato purée into the pan. Scrape up any bits stuck to the bottom, then tip into the slow cooker, cover and cook on low for 6 hrs. Cool completely if freezing.

Nutrition per serving
kcal 447 • fat 27g • saturates 8g •carbs 7g • sugars 6g • fibre 4g • protein 34g • salt 2.9g

Goan pulled pork

Cooked long and slow, the spices and vinegar mellow to create tender, full-flavoured pork, which you can then shred and wrap up with salad and raita in chapatis.

EASY ⏱ PREP 15 mins COOK 8 hrs 15 mins 🕐 SERVES 6

- 2 tbsp olive oil
- 1 large onion, halved and sliced
- 1 garlic bulb, cloves peeled
- thumb-sized piece ginger, shredded into very thin matchsticks
- 1 tbsp ground cumin
- 2 tbsp each smoked paprika and ground coriander
- ½-1 tsp cayenne pepper (depending on how hot you like it)
- 225ml cider vinegar
- 2kg boneless pork leg or shoulder

FOR THE SALAD
- 3 carrots, shredded with a julienne peeler or coarsely grated
- 1 red onion, finely chopped
- 3 tomatoes, chopped
- generous handful coriander
- juice 1 lemon
- 1 tbsp olive oil

TO SERVE
- 12 warm chapatis or small wraps, chunky cucumber raita and mango chutney

1 Heat the oil in a large frying pan. Fry the onion, garlic and ginger for about 10 mins. Stir in the spices, pour in the vinegar and stir well. Tip into a slow cooker (we used a 6.5-litre model) and add 1 tsp salt and about 20 turns of a black pepper mill. Add the pork joint, turn in the mixture to coat it, then arrange it in the pot so it is rind-side down. Cover and cook on low for 7–8 hrs. Cool and transfer to a freezerproof container; freeze for up to 3 months.

2 Meanwhile, make the salad. Mix the carrot with the onion, tomato and coriander, then toss just before serving with the lemon juice and oil.

3 Remove the rind and fat from the pork and skim all the fat from the juices, then shred the meat into the juices. To serve, put some meat and salad on one side of a chapati, then top with the raita and chutney, fold over and eat with your hands.

Nutrition per serving
kcal 529 • fat 24g • saturates 7g •carbs 11g • sugars 9g • fibre 7g • protein 65g • salt 1.1g

Spicy pies with sweet potato mash

This mince recipe is loosely based on the classic American sloppy joe, which is often served in a bun. We've topped it with mash instead to make a great alternative to cottage pie.

EASY 🕐 PREP 20 mins COOK 40 mins 🕐 MAKES 6

FOR THE MASH
- 1 kg sweet potatoes, peeled and cut into large chunks
- 2 tbsp milk
- 50g mature cheddar, finely grated

FOR THE MINCE
- 1 tbsp rapeseed oil
- 2 onions, halved and sliced
- 500g lean beef mince (5% fat)
- 1 tbsp smoked paprika, plus extra for sprinkling
- 1 tbsp ground cumin
- 1 tbsp ground coriander
- 1 tbsp mild chilli powder
- 1 tbsp vegetable bouillon powder
- 400g can black-eyed beans
- 400g can chopped tomatoes
- 1 large green pepper, diced
- 326g can sweetcorn in water
- broccoli or salad, to serve (optional)

1 Boil the sweet potato for 15 mins or until tender, taking care not to overcook.

2 Meanwhile, heat the oil in a large, deep, non-stick frying pan. Add the onions, cover and cook for 8 mins or until softened and starting to colour. Stir in the mince, breaking it up with a wooden spoon until browned. Stir in all the spices and bouillon, then add the beans with their liquid, the tomatoes and pepper. Cover and simmer for 20 mins. Stir in the corn with its liquid, season and take off the heat.

3 While the mince cooks, mash the potatoes with the milk to make a stiff mash. Spoon the mince into 6 individual pie dishes, top each with some mash, then sprinkle over the cheese and a little paprika.

4 The pies can now be frozen. If eating straight away, put under a hot grill until piping hot and the cheese is melted. To cook from frozen, thaw completely, then reheat in the oven on a baking tray at 180C/160C fan/gas 4 for about 30–40 mins or until piping hot throughout. Serve with broccoli or a salad, if you like, which will take you to all 5 of your 5-a-day.

Nutrition per pie
kcal 452 • fat 11g • saturates 4g • carbs 52g • sugars 23g • fibre 13g • protein 29g • salt 0.8g

Easy pulled beef ragu

This is one of those low-and-slow cooking dishes that works a treat when you don't have time to be in the kitchen stirring. Just add this rich sauce and tender shredded beef to your favourite robust pasta.

EASY ⏱ PREP 20 mins COOK 4 hrs ◔ SERVES 8 (OR 2 MEALS FOR 4)

- 2 tbsp olive oil
- 1kg boneless beef brisket
- 2 onions, finely chopped
- 4 garlic cloves, finely chopped
- 5 carrots, thickly sliced
- 250ml red wine
- 2 x 400g cans chopped tomatoes
- 2 tbsp tomato purée
- 4 bay leaves
- 450g large pasta shapes (such as paccheri, rigate or rigatoni)
- large handful basil leaves, to serve
- grated Parmesan, to serve

1 Heat oven to 150C/130C fan/gas 2. Heat 1 tbsp oil in a flameproof casserole dish and brown the beef all over. Take the beef out of the dish, add the remaining oil and gently cook the onions and garlic for 10 mins until softened.

2 Add the browned beef back to the dish with the carrots, red wine, tomatoes, tomato purée and bay leaves. Cover with foil and a lid, and slowly cook for 3–3½ hrs or until the meat falls apart. Check on it a couple of times, turning the beef over and giving it a good stir to make sure it's coated in the sauce.

3 Cook the pasta following pack instructions, then drain. Shred the beef – it should just fall apart when you touch it with a fork – then spoon the beef and tomato sauce over the pasta or cool and transfer to a freezerproof container; freeze for up to 3 months. Scatter with basil and Parmesan before serving.

Nutrition per serving
kcal 543 • fat 18g • saturates 6g •carbs 54g • sugars 10g • fibre 6g • protein 32g • salt 0.1g

Green burgers

This recipe has been designed so you can stash an extra family meal in the freezer, and they're packed with spinach, which can be one of the trickier vegetables to get kids to eat. They're ideal if you're feeding your family at different times.

EASY ⏱ PREP 30 mins COOK 20 mins ⏲ MAKES 8 (4 FOR NOW, 4 FOR THE FREEZER)

- 2 tbsp olive oil
- 2 onions, finely chopped
- 250g bag spinach
- 5 slices white bread, blitzed into breadcrumbs (or 150g dried breadcrumbs)
- good grating of fresh nutmeg
- 100g mature cheddar, grated
- 40g Parmesan, finely grated
- 1–2 large eggs, beaten
- 3 tbsp plain flour

TO SERVE
- 6 crusty bread rolls
- 4 ripe, juicy tomatoes, thickly sliced
- good-quality ketchup or other relish
- sweet potato fries (optional)

1 Heat half the oil in a frying pan and gently fry the onions for about 10 mins until pale and soft, then leave to cool a little.
2 Finely chop the spinach in a food processor and tip into a bowl. Add the cooled onion, breadcrumbs, nutmeg, cheddar and Parmesan, and mash together. Add the beaten egg, a little at a time (you may not need all of it), until the mixture holds together. Divide into 8 and shape into fat burgers.
3 Put the flour in a shallow bowl, season well and dip the burgers into the flour to coat. Store in a plastic container between layers of baking parchment. Either chill until ready to cook, or freeze.
4 Heat the remaining oil in the frying pan and fry the burgers for about 5 mins each side until browned all over. Serve in the crusty rolls, with a couple of slices of tomato, ketchup and sweet potato fries on the side, if you like.

Nutrition per burger
kcal 233 • fat 11g • saturates 5g • carbs 22g • sugars 3g • fibre 1g • protein 11g • salt 0.5g

Pull-apart pork with honey chipotle

Melt-in-the-mouth, tender shredded pork with a sweet and spicy glaze, what's not to like? Serve this simple make-ahead meal with all the trimmings.

EASY ⏲ PREP 10 mins plus marinating COOK 4 hrs 30 mins ⌷ SERVES 8

- 75g ketchup, plus 1 tbsp
- 3 tbsp chipotle paste
- 3 tbsp honey
- 1 tbsp red wine vinegar
- 1.2kg trimmed pork shoulder joint (weight after cutting away the rind – ask your butcher to do this)

1 Up to 2 days before (and at least 2 hrs ahead), mix together 75g ketchup with 2 tbsp chipotle, 2 tbsp honey and the vinegar. Rub all over the pork and leave in a food bag (or bowl) in the fridge to marinate, turning occasionally.

2 Heat oven to 160C/140C fan/gas 3. Lift the pork into a snug-fitting roasting tin and baste with any excess marinade, plus 100ml water. Cover with foil, ensuring the pork is sealed in but the foil isn't touching it, and bake for 4 hrs.

3 Turn up the oven to 200C/180C fan/gas 6 (or cool and chill the pork, if making ahead). Remove the foil and put the pork back in for 30 mins until crisp and sticky on the outside.

4 Lift the pork from the tin and use 2 forks to shred the meat. Mix together the extra 1 tbsp ketchup with the remaining chipotle and honey, and stir it through the shredded meat with some seasoning before serving. The pork can be frozen in batches; defrost thoroughly and heat through before serving.

Nutrition per serving
kcal 267 • fat 10g • saturates 3g • carbs 9g • sugars 9g • fibre none • protein 35g • salt 0.5g

Italian veggie cottage pie

An Italian twist on an English classic, with sundried tomato, spinach and aubergine, this veggie pie makes a super budget supper.

EASY · PREP 10 mins COOK 30 mins · SERVES 6

- 4 tbsp olive oil
- 2 aubergines, cut into chunks
- 2 large garlic cloves, crushed
- 16 sundried tomatoes, roughly chopped, plus 1 tbsp of their oil
- 2 tsp dried oregano
- 400g spinach, washed
- 50g plain flour
- 400ml milk
- 125g cheddar, grated, plus extra to top
- 800g ready-made mashed potatoes

1 Heat the oven to 220C/200C fan/gas 7. Heat 1 tbsp of the oil in a large, lidded frying pan or flameproof casserole dish. Cook the aubergine, in 2 batches, over a high heat for 4–5 mins until golden, adding extra oil as you need to. Return all the aubergine to the pan with the garlic, tomatoes and 1½ tsp oregano and cook for 1 min. Stir in the spinach, put the lid on the pan and leave for a few mins to wilt.

2 Add the flour and stir through until combined. Pour in the milk, stir gently and bring to the boil. Bubble for a few mins, then stir in the cheese and season. Cook until the cheese has melted and the sauce has thickened.

3 Mix the mash with the remaining oregano and spread over the filling. Scatter over a little more grated cheese and bake for 10–15 mins until golden. Can be frozen before or after baking.

Nutrition per serving
kcal 432 · fat 24g · saturates 10g · carbs 35g · sugars 9g · fibre 8g · protein 15g · salt 0.7g

Artichoke, aubergine & lamb moussaka

You can use freshly cooked artichokes here, but it makes this an expensive dish. When you use canned, it's best to drain them really well, blotting them with kitchen paper to soak up the excess brine. For added flavour, halve them and marinate in extra virgin olive oil with thyme and sliced garlic for a couple of days, then drain. You can use the oil for cooking the lamb and onions.

MORE EFFORT ⏱ PREP 40 mins COOK 1 hr 40 mins ◷ SERVES 8–10

- olive oil, for frying
- 1kg lamb mince
- 2 large onions, finely chopped
- 3 garlic cloves, chopped
- 2 x 395g cans cherry tomatoes in thick juice
- 2 bay leaves
- 1 cinnamon stick
- ½ tsp dried oregano
- pinch of sugar
- 2 medium aubergines, cut into rounds
- 700g large potatoes, thinly sliced
- 2 x 390g cans artichoke hearts, drained really well (see above)

FOR THE SAUCE
- 100g butter
- 100g plain flour
- 900ml milk
- very generous grating of nutmeg
- 125g grated Gruyère
- 25g grated Parmesan
- 3 medium eggs, lightly beaten

1 Heat 1½ tbsp oil in a heavy-based pan until hot, then fry the lamb until golden, about 10 mins. Remove with a slotted spoon and set aside. Pour off all but 2 tbsp oil and fry the onion until soft and golden. Add the garlic and cook for a few mins, then add tomatoes, bay, cinnamon, oregano, sugar and seasoning. Bring to the boil, turn down to simmer, then return the meat, cover and cook for 40 mins over a low heat. Uncover and cook to a thick sauce.

2 Heat 2 tbsp oil in 1 or 2 frying pans and cook the aubergine in batches until golden, then turn down the heat and cook until soft. Season and remove. Add a little oil and cook the potatoes in batches, on both sides, until pale gold, adding more oil and removing as you go. Season and set aside.

3 Fry the artichoke hearts in olive oil over a high heat to get some colour, but be careful they don't fall apart. Season.

4 Remove the bay and cinnamon from the meat and season. Layer up the moussaka in a roughly 32 x 23 x 6cm dish. Put potato in the bottom, then half the meat. Put aubergine on top, then the rest of the meat. Spoon the artichokes on top.

5 Heat oven to 200C/180C fan/gas 6. To make the sauce, melt the butter in a heavy-based pan and stir in the flour until it becomes dry and sandy coloured. Take off the heat and add the milk, a little at a time. Beat well after each addition until smooth. Put back on the heat and bring to the boil, stirring, until it thickens to form a sauce.

6 Add nutmeg, salt and pepper. Turn down the heat and cook for 5 mins. Add three-quarters of the cheese and season. Leave to cool a little, then beat in the eggs. Pour over the dish and scatter the remaining cheese on top. Bake for 30 mins until brown and bubbling. Leave to cool for 10 mins. Will freeze; defrost thoroughly before reheating.

Nutrition per serving (10)
kcal 588 • fat 33g • saturates 17g • carbs 35g • sugars 15g • fibre 7g • protein 34g • salt 1.0g

Beef & red pepper burgers

Pack your patties with extra vegetables – carrot and roasted pepper – to boost flavour and up your veggie intake.

EASY 🕐 PREP 30 mins COOK 40 mins ⟲ MAKES 6

- 1 red pepper, cut into quarters
- 2 tbsp olive oil
- 400g lean steak mince
- 1 medium egg
- 1 carrot, coarsely grated
- 50g stale breadcrumbs
- 40g cheddar, finely sliced

TO SERVE
- 6 floury rolls, halved
- 3 tbsp mayonnaise
- ¼ cucumber, or 1–2 mini cucumbers, sliced

1 Heat oven to 200C/180C fan/gas 6. Put the pepper on a baking tray and rub with ½ tbsp oil. Roast in the oven for 25–30 mins, turning once halfway through. Remove and allow to cool slightly before finely chopping.

2 Tip the mince, roasted pepper, egg, carrot and breadcrumbs into a large bowl and mix well. Using your hands, shape the mixture into 6 equal burgers. Freeze if you like, wrapping each burger separately.

3 Heat the remaining oil in a large, heavy-based, non-stick frying pan over a medium heat. Fry the burgers for 5–6 mins each side until cooked through. Top with slices of cheddar. Spread the rolls with mayo, add the burgers and top with slices of cucumber.

Nutrition per serving
kcal 199 • fat 10g • saturates 4g • carbs 9g • sugars 3g • fibre 1g • protein 18g • salt 0.4g

Chilli con carne

A warm, comforting chilli is the ultimate family meal. This dish is great for all seasons and has a mix of sweet (cascabel) and smoky (ancho) chillis to give it depth.

A LITTLE EFFORT ⏱ PREP 30 mins COOK 4 hrs 45 mins ◷ SERVES 6-8

- 80ml olive oil
- 2 large onions, roughly chopped
- 2 large dried ancho chillies
- 3 dried cascabel chillies
- 2 tsp smoked paprika
- 2 tsp dried thyme
- 3 celery sticks, finely chopped
- 1 beef stock cube
- 1.5kg beef shin, boneless and cut into large chunks
- 1 tbsp plain flour
- 3 carrots, trimmed, left whole
- 50ml maple syrup
- 1 can chopped tomatoes
- 500ml bottle dark beer
- 500ml fresh beef stock
- coriander sprigs, to serve

1 Heat oven to 160C/140C fan/gas 3. Heat a large cast-iron pot or saucepan over a high flame, pour in the oil, then drop in the onions, chillies, paprika and thyme. Cook for 5 mins until the onions soften. Add the celery, give it a stir and crumble in the stock cube. Stir again and cook for another 5 mins.

2 Add the beef, stir well, then colour for a few mins to coat the meat with the spices. Add the flour and coat everything with a few more stirs, then add the remaining ingredients, along with 1 tsp salt.

3 Let it come to the boil, then put a lid on, place in the oven, reduce the temperature to 140C/120C fan/gas 1 and cook for 4½ hrs.

4 Take the pot out of the oven and remove the carrots, chop them into small chunks, then put them back in. I like plenty of sauce, but you may want to remove some if you don't want it too saucy – be sure to keep it, it's great on toast when cold. Remember to remove the chillies before you serve. Cool and transfer to a freezerproof container; freeze for up to 3 months, Finally, scatter with coriander, if you like, before serving.

Nutrition per serving (8)
kcal 449 • fat 22g • saturates 6g • carbs 17g • sugars 13g • fibre 4g • protein 38g • salt 1.3g

Peppered mackerel fish cakes

Use up leftover mash to create a comforting, good-value family meal.

EASY ⏱ PREP 20 mins COOK 15 mins ⏲ SERVES 4

- 300g cold mashed potato
- 6 spring onions, thinly sliced
- 1 tbsp horseradish sauce
- 250g peppered mackerel fillets, skinned and flaked
- 2 tbsp plain flour
- 1 egg, beaten
- 85g dried breadcrumbs
- sunflower oil, for frying (optional)
- salad and lemon wedges, to serve

1 In a large bowl, mix together the potato, spring onions, horseradish and mackerel, then shape into 8 even-size cakes. Roll the fish cakes in the flour, shaking off any excess, then dip in the egg, followed by the breadcrumbs. Cover and chill until ready to cook. The fish cakes can be prepared and chilled up to a day ahead, or frozen – separate each one with a piece of parchment paper first.
2 Gently grill or shallow-fry the fish cakes for 5–6 mins on each side until crunchy, golden brown and hot all the way through. Serve with salad and lemon wedges.

Nutrition per serving
kcals 427 • 26g fat • 5g saturates • 32g carbs • 2g sugars • 2g fibre • 18g protein • 1.76g salt

Venison sausage & chestnut casserole

This warming sausage stew is a perfect make-ahead main, with a rich red wine sauce, chestnuts and a creamy mustard mash.

EASY 🕐 PREP 15 mins COOK 1 hr ⏱ SERVES 8

- 2 tbsp sunflower oil
- 16 venison sausages
- 2 medium onions, thinly sliced
- 3 celery sticks, trimmed and thinly sliced
- 200g chestnut mushrooms, halved (or quartered if large)
- 300ml red wine
- 1 beef stock cube
- 200g pack vacuum-packed cooked chestnuts
- 2 tbsp tomato purée
- 1 bay leaf
- 2 tbsp cornflour
- small pack parsley, chopped, to serve (optional)

FOR THE MUSTARD MASH
- 1.5kg medium potatoes (ideally Maris Piper), cut into even chunks
- 75g butter
- 150ml tub double cream
- 2 tbsp wholegrain mustard

1 Heat 1 tbsp of the oil in a large non-stick frying pan and fry the sausages in 2 batches over a medium heat for 15 mins, turning regularly, until nicely browned. Transfer the sausages to a large flameproof casserole dish.

2 Tip the onions and celery into the frying pan and cook over a medium-high heat for 5 mins or until beginning to soften and lightly colour, stirring regularly. Add a splash more oil if needed. Tip the vegetables into the casserole dish.

3 Put the remaining oil in the pan, cook the mushrooms over a high heat for 4–5 mins until lightly browned, then add to the casserole. Pour the wine and 300ml water into the dish and crumble the stock cube over the top. Stir in the chestnuts, tomato purée and bay leaf. Bring to the boil, then reduce the heat, cover loosely with a lid and simmer gently for 30 mins, stirring occasionally.

4 Meanwhile, make the mustard mash. Put the potatoes in a large pan of water, bring to the boil, then reduce the heat and simmer for 15–20 mins or until the potatoes are soft but not falling apart. Drain well in a colander, then return to the pan and mash with the butter and cream until smooth. Beat in the mustard, season to taste, and set aside.

5 Mix the cornflour with 2 tbsp cold water until smooth. Stir into the casserole and cook for 2–3 mins, stirring regularly, until the sauce has thickened. Remove the dish from the heat, season and sprinkle with chopped parsley, if using. Serve with the mustard mash. Can be frozen for up to 3 months, defrost thoroughly and reheat until piping hot.

Nutrition: per serving
kcal 591 • fat 27g • saturates 14g • carbs 52g • sugars 7g • fibre 7g • protein 25g • salt 1.8g

Cottage pie

This great-value family favourite freezes beautifully and is a guaranteed crowd-pleaser.

EASY ⏱ PREP 35 mins COOK 1 hr 50 mins ⏱ SERVES 10

- 3 tbsp olive oil
- 1.25kg beef mince
- 2 onions, finely chopped
- 3 carrots, chopped
- 3 celery sticks, chopped
- 2 garlic cloves, finely chopped
- 3 tbsp plain flour
- 1 tbsp tomato purée
- large glass red wine (optional)
- 850ml beef stock
- 4 tbsp Worcestershire sauce
- few thyme sprigs
- 2 bay leaves

FOR THE MASH
- 1.8kg potatoes, chopped
- 225ml milk
- 25g butter
- 200g strong cheddar, grated
- freshly grated nutmeg

1 Heat 1 tbsp oil in a large saucepan and fry the mince until browned – you may need to do this in batches. Set aside as it browns. Put the rest of the oil into the pan, add the vegetables and cook on a gentle heat until soft, about 20 mins. Add the garlic, flour and tomato purée, increase the heat and cook for a few mins, then return the beef to the pan. Pour over the wine, if using, and boil to reduce it slightly before adding the stock, Worcestershire sauce and herbs. Bring to a simmer and cook, uncovered, for 45 mins. By this time the gravy should be thick and coating the meat. Check after about 30 mins – if a lot of liquid remains, increase the heat slightly to reduce the gravy a little. Season well, then discard the bay leaves and thyme stalks.

2 Meanwhile, make the mash. In a large saucepan, cover the potatoes in salted cold water, bring to the boil and simmer until tender. Drain well, then allow to steam-dry for a few mins. Mash well with the milk, butter, and three-quarters of the cheese, then season with the nutmeg and some salt and pepper.

3 Spoon the meat into 2 ovenproof dishes. Pipe or spoon on the mash to cover. Sprinkle on the remaining cheese. If eating straight away, heat oven to 220C/200C fan/gas 7 and cook for 25–30 mins, or until the topping is golden. To freeze, make sure the pie is completely cold, then cover it well with cling film and freeze. Defrost in the fridge overnight, then cook as per the recipe. Alternatively, to cook from frozen, heat the oven to 180C/160C fan/gas 4, cover with foil and cook for 1½ hrs. Increase the oven to 220C/200C fan/gas 7, uncover and cook for 20 mins more, until golden and bubbling.

Nutrition per serving
kcal 600 • fat 34g • saturates 16g • carbs 40g • sugars 7g • fibre 4g • protein 37g • salt 1.15g

Easy fish cakes

These freezable and simple-to-make fish patties are ideal as a family meal or can be made and frozen individually as a quick last-minute kids' supper for any age.

EASY 🕐 PREP 15 mins plus chilling COOK 40 mins 🕐 SERVES 4–6 OR MAKES 6–8 TODDLER MEALS

- 450g potatoes, peeled, large ones cut in half
- knob of butter
- 1 x pack fish pie mix (cod, salmon, smoked haddock etc, weight around 320g-400g depending on pack size)
- 3 spring onions, finely chopped
- 100ml milk
- 75g frozen sweetcorn, defrosted
- handful of grated cheddar cheese
- 1 large egg, beaten
- flour, for dusting
- olive oil, for frying

1 Cook the potatoes in boiling water until just tender. Drain well and return to the pan on a low heat. Heat for another minute or two to evaporate excess liquid. Mash the potato with a small knob of butter. Allow to cool.

2 Put the fish, spring onions and milk in a shallow dish, cover with cling film and cook in the microwave for 1–2 mins until just cooked. If you don't have a microwave, put everything in a saucepan and gently cook until just opaque and cooked through.

3 Drain the fish and spring onions through a fine sieve. Gently mix through the potatoes, avoiding breaking up the fish too much, along with the sweetcorn, cheddar and a generous grind of black pepper. Form into 6–8 patties. The cooler the mash potato is when you do this, the easier it will be to form the patties as the mixture will be very soft when warm.

4 Pour the egg on one plate and scatter flour on the other. Dip the patties in egg and then flour and arrange on a sheet of baking paper on a tray. Put the patties in the fridge for at least half an hour to firm up if the patties feel very soft. At this point you can freeze the patties, wrapped individually. Defrost throughly before moving onto the next stage.

5 Heat a large frying pan with a generous glug of olive oil. When the oil is hot, carefully lower the fish cakes into the pan. Cook for 5–7 minutes or until golden brown underneath and then carefully flip them over. Fry for another 5–7 minutes or until golden on the bottom and heated all the way through.

Nutrition per serving (4)
kcal 352 • fat 18,4 g • saturates 5g • carbs 23,7g • sugars 2,5g • fibre 2,5g • protein 22,5g • salt 0,7 g

Easy beef stew with sweet potato topping

Perfect for the whole family, this freezable pie makes a great meal for toddlers and teens alike and has plenty of veg.

EASY ⏱ PREP 15 mins COOK 2 hrs 30 mins 🕐 SERVES 4

- 1 tbsp olive oil
- 1 onion, finely chopped
- 2 carrots, finely diced (about 130g)
- 1–2 sticks celery, finely diced (about 130g)
- 400-500g braising steak
- 2 fat garlic cloves, crushed
- 1 tsp ground cinnamon
- 1 low-salt beef stock cube
- 2 tbsp tomato purée
- 1 x 25g pack parsley, stalks and leaves finely chopped separately
- 1kg sweet potatoes, peeled and diced
- knob of butter
- handful grated cheddar

1 Heat the olive oil in a heavy-based pan. Add the onions and cook for 2 mins, then add the carrot and celery and cook until softened. Add a little water if the mixture sticks.

2 Add the braising steak and cook until browned, then stir in the garlic and cinnamon and cook for a further 1–2 mins until the aromas are released.

3 Add the stock cube to 500ml boiling water and stir into the meat, along with the tomato purée and parsley stalks. Bring to the boil and simmer, covered, for 1 hour, then take off the lid and simmer for another hour or until the meat is very tender. Stir in the chopped parsley leaves.

4 Transfer the stew into a medium-sized ceramic dish (that would be big enough for 4 adults), or into 6–8 large ramekins for make-ahead kids' portions.

5 Meanwhile, steam or boil the sweet potatoes until tender. Preheat the oven to 200C/180C fan/gas mark 6. Drain the potatoes well and mash with the butter. Spoon on top of the meat, sprinkle with the cheese and cook on the top shelf for around 20 minutes until golden and bubbling. Alternatively, cover and freeze the pie or mini pies for another time. Defrost thoroughly before cooking – you can do this by leaving it in the fridge overnight if you like. Cook for around 30–35 mins or until golden, bubbling and hot throughout.

Nutrition per serving
kcal 474 • fat 14.1 g • saturates 5.7g • carbs 56g • sugars 19g • fibre 10.9g • protein 31.2g • salt 1.4 g

Spaghetti & meatballs

Get everyone to help rolling meatballs and you'll soon have one supper on the table and another in the freezer.

EASY · PREP 30 mins COOK 30 mins · SERVES 10

- 8 good-quality pork sausages
- 1kg beef mince
- 1 onion, finely chopped
- ½ a large bunch flat-leaf parsley, finely chopped
- 85g Parmesan, grated, plus extra to serve if you like
- 100g fresh breadcrumbs
- 2 eggs, beaten with a fork
- olive oil, for roasting
- spaghetti, to serve (you'll need about 100g per portion)

FOR THE SAUCE
- 3 tbsp olive oil
- 4 garlic cloves, crushed
- 4 x 400g cans chopped tomatoes
- 125ml red wine (optional)
- 3 tbsp caster sugar
- ½ a large bunch flat-leaf parsley, finely chopped
- few basil leaves (optional)

1 First make the meatballs. Split the sausage skins and squeeze out the meat into your largest mixing bowl. Add the mince, onion, parsley, Parmesan, breadcrumbs, beaten eggs and lots of seasoning. Get your hands in and mix together really well – the more you squeeze and mash the mince, the more tender the meatballs will be.

2 Heat oven to 220C/200C fan/gas 7. Roll the mince mixture into about 50 golf-ball-size meatballs. Set aside any meatballs for freezing, allowing about 5 per portion, then spread the rest out in a large roasting tin – the meatballs will brown better if spaced out a bit. Drizzle with a little oil (about 1 tsp per portion), shake to coat, then roast for 20–30 mins until browned.

3 Meanwhile, make the sauce. Heat the oil in your largest pan. Add the garlic and sizzle for 1 min. Stir in the tomatoes, wine, if using, sugar, parsley and seasoning. Simmer for 15–20 mins until slightly thickened. Stir in the basil leaves, if using, spoon out any portions for freezing, then add the cooked meatballs to the pan to keep warm while you boil the spaghetti. Spoon the sauce and meatballs over spaghetti, or stir them all together and serve with extra Parmesan and a few basil leaves, if you like. To freeze separately, put the sauce in freezer bags, but open-freeze the uncooked meatballs on a tray, then wrap well in cling film once hard. To cook, defrost meatballs and cook as above, or roast from frozen at 180C/160C fan/gas 4 for 30 mins, then shake and increase oven to 220C/200C fan/gas 7 for 10 mins more. Defrost sauce and bring to a simmer in a pan before serving. To freeze together, mix the roasted meatballs into the sauce and freeze in portions. Defrost thoroughly overnight in the fridge, then heat in a covered pan until the sauce and meatballs are piping hot.

Nutrition per serving
kcal 870 • fat 37g • saturates 13g • carbs 95g • sugars 13g • fibre 5g • protein 46g • salt 1.34g

Sausage & bean casserole

Dish up a hearty bowl of comfort on a cold, wintry evening with this simple sausage stew.

EASY ⏱ PREP 15 mins COOK 50 mins ⏲ SERVES 4

- 1 tbsp vegetable oil
- 8 pork sausages
- 2 celery sticks, chopped
- 2 carrots, chopped
- 1 onion, chopped
- 1 tbsp tomato purée
- 400g can butter beans
- 400g can baked beans in tomato sauce
- ½ small bunch thyme
- 200ml hot chicken or veg stock
- 2 slices white bread, whizzed to crumbs

1 Heat half the oil in a large casserole dish, then brown the sausages all over. Remove from the pan and set aside. Add the remaining oil, tip the veg into the dish and fry for 10 mins. Stir in the tomato purée and cook for 1 min more.

2 Heat oven to 200C/180C fan/gas 6. Return the sausages to the pan with the beans, thyme and some seasoning, then pour in the stock and bring to a simmer. Remove from the heat, sprinkle over the breadcrumbs, then bake in the oven for 25–30 mins until the crumbs are golden and the stew is bubbling. To freeze, cool completely and wrap well in cling film.

Nutrition per serving
kcal 580 • fat 33g • saturates 10g • carbs 50g • sugars 16g • fibre 10g • protein 25g • salt 3.85g

Sausage, bean & cheese pasties

Only 5 ingredients and perfect for freezing ahead, these tasty pasties make a very handy stand-by.

EASY 🕐 PREP 30 mins plus rising COOK 30 mins 🥧 MAKES 12

- 500g pack bread mix
- 8 sausages
- 2 x 420g cans baked beans
- 140g cheddar, grated
- 1 egg, beaten

1 Prepare the bread mix following pack instructions. While the dough rises, make the filling. Skin the sausages and roll the meat into small meatballs, about 6–8 per sausage. Heat a large deep frying pan and brown the sausages. You may need to do this in batches. Once they're all brown, return them to the pan and pour in the beans. Mix to combine, then allow the mix to cool a little while you roll the dough.

2 Heat oven to 200C/180C fan/gas 6. Grease 2 or 3 large, flat baking sheets. Divide the dough into 12 and roll out each one to a circle, roughly 17cm in diameter – and keep the remaining balls of dough covered with oiled cling film or a damp tea towel.

3 Taking each circle in turn, fill with a scoop of the bean mix and a little of the grated cheese. Fold in half, pressing well to seal. Crimp the edges then transfer to an oiled baking tray. Keep covered with oiled cling film while you make the rest. Brush with a little beaten egg and cook for 15–20 mins until puffed up and golden.

4 Remove and allow to cool slightly on a wire rack. Eat warm or at room temperature. If you would like to freeze the pasties, completely cool and freeze in a single layer on a flat tray, covered well. Once frozen, transfer them to a freezer bag and seal well. Allow to defrost overnight in the fridge or for 4–5 hrs at room temperature. Reheat in a hot oven for 10 mins until piping hot.

Nutrition per serving
kcal 348 • fat 16g • saturates 6g • carbs 38g • sugars 6g • fibre 5g • protein 16g • salt 2.4g

Chilli bean bake with soured cream mash

A comforting supper for a crowd that you can freeze ahead to save time on the night.

EASY 🕐 PREP 20 mins COOK 1 hr 20 mins ⏱ SERVES 10

- 2 onions, chopped
- 1 tbsp olive oil
- 2 tsp each ground cumin and dried thyme
- 2 tbsp mild chilli powder
- 1kg lean minced beef
- 2 x 400g cans chopped tomatoes
- 2 x 400g cans kidney beans, rinsed and drained
- 2 x 330g cans sweetcorn, drained
- 3 mixed peppers, chopped into chunks
- 2 tbsp white or red wine vinegar
- 2 tbsp brown sugar
- 1 beef stock cube

FOR THE MASH
- 1.8kg potatoes, chopped into large chunks
- 300ml pot soured cream
- 2 x small bunches chives, snipped
- 100g cheddar, grated

1 Fry the onions in the oil in a large, deep saucepan until soft. Stir in the spices and cook for 2 mins, until fragrant. Crumble in the mince in batches and fry, breaking up with a wooden spoon, until all the meat is browned.

2 Stir in the chopped tomatoes, beans, sweetcorn, peppers, vinegar and sugar. Crumble in the stock cube, pour over 500ml water then bring to the boil. Cover and simmer for 20 mins, then uncover and simmer for 20 mins more until the mince and peppers are tender and saucy.

3 Meanwhile, make the mash. Boil the potatoes in lots of boiling salted water until tender, about 15 mins. Drain well, leaving in the colander to steam dry for 1 min, then tip back into the saucepan and mash with the soured cream. Season and stir in the chives.

4 When the chilli mince is done, pour into 1, 2 or individual ovenproof dishes. Spoon or pipe over the mash and scatter on the cheese. Cool completely if you're freezing any at this stage, or if you want to eat straight away, heat the oven to 220C/200C fan/gas 7 and bake for 25–30 mins until bubbling and golden.

Nutrition per serving
kcal 599 • fat 23g • saturates 11g • carbs 66g • sugars 17g • fibre 8g • protein 37g • salt 1.92g

Lentil & lamb moussaka

More lentils, less mince is the key to this low-cost family meal.

EASY ⏱ PREP 15 mins COOK 40 mins 🕒 SERVES 6

- 1 tbsp olive oil
- 1 onion, chopped
- 1 garlic clove, crushed
- 1 aubergine, diced
- 250g lean minced lamb
- 400g can lentils in water, drained
- 400g can chopped tomatoes
- 500g cooked potatoes, diced
- 2 tsp dried oregano
- ½ tsp cinnamon
- 150ml hot vegetable stock
- 500g tub Greek yogurt
- 1 egg, beaten

1 Heat the oil in a large frying pan. Add the onion and cook for 3 mins until starting to colour and soften.
2 Add the garlic, aubergine and minced lamb, then cook for 5–10 mins until the mince is brown and the aubergine is softened.
3 Stir in the lentils, tomatoes, potatoes, oregano, cinnamon, some seasoning and the stock.
4 Increase the heat and simmer for 10–15 mins until the mixture thickens.
5 Heat a grill to high. Transfer the lentil and lamb mix to an ovenproof dish. Mix the Greek yogurt with the beaten egg, then pour on top of the lentil and lamb mix. Grill for 5 mins until the top is bubbling and golden.

Nutrition per serving
kcal 343 • fat 17g • saturates 9g • carbs 29g • sugar 8g • fibre 6g • protein 20g • salt 0.59g

Cheeseburgers

Keep the kids happy with these wallet-friendly cheeseburgers – ready in just 35 minutes and you can freeze leftovers.

EASY 🕐 PREP 15 mins COOK 20 mins 🕒 MAKES 12

- 1kg beef mince
- 300g breadcrumbs
- 140g extra-mature or mature cheddar, grated
- 4 tbsp Worcestershire sauce
- 1 small bunch parsley, finely chopped
- 2 eggs, beaten

TO SERVE
- split burger buns
- sliced tomatoes
- red onion slices
- lettuce
- tomato sauce
- coleslaw
- wedges or fries

1 Crumble the mince in a large bowl, then tip in the breadcrumbs, cheese, Worcestershire sauce, parsley and eggs with 1 tsp ground pepper and 1–2 tsp salt. Mix with your hands to combine everything thoroughly.

2 Shape the mix into 12 burgers. Chill until ready to cook for up to 24 hrs. Or freeze for up to 3 months. Just stack between squares of baking parchment to stop the burgers sticking together, then wrap well. Defrost overnight in the fridge before cooking.

3 To cook the burgers, heat a grill to high. Grill the burgers for 6–8 mins on each side until cooked through. Meanwhile, warm as many buns as you need in a foil-covered tray below the grilling burgers. Let everyone assemble their own, served with their favourite accompaniments.

Nutrition per burger
kcal 343 • fat 19g • saturates 9g • carbs 20g • sugars 1g • fibre 1g • protein 24g • salt 1.05g

Bacon, spinach & Gorgonzola pasta

An indulgent pasta dish that is quick and cheap to make.

EASY ⏱ PREP 10 mins COOK 15 mins ◔ SERVES 4

- 350g penne pasta
- 1 tbsp vegetable oil
- 1 onion, chopped
- 8 rashers smoked bacon, chopped
- 200ml hot vegetable stock
- 300g frozen peas
- 150g pack Gorgonzola, cubed
- 250g spinach

1 Cook the pasta following pack instructions. Meanwhile, heat the oil in a large frying pan, then add the onion and cook for 3 mins until starting to soften. Add the bacon, cook for a further 5 mins, then pour in the hot stock and bring to the boil. Simmer for a few mins until the liquid has reduced slightly.

2 Stir in the peas, followed by the Gorgonzola, until the cheese has melted and the peas are defrosted. Quickly stir through the spinach to wilt. Drain the pasta and mix with the sauce, then serve. Can be frozen at this point for up to one month. Freeze it in a baking dish and reheat, covered, in the oven.

Nutrition per serving
kcal 658 • fat 25g • saturates 11g • carbs 77g • sugars 7g • fibre 9g • protein 35g • salt 4.06g

Chicken, leek & parsley pie

Making two pies is nowhere near double the work, so it's worth making an extra one to freeze.

EASY 🕐 PREP 2 hrs COOK 30 mins 🕐 SERVES 2 ADULTS AND 4 KIDS

- 1.4kg chicken
- 1 each carrot, onion and celery stick
- 1 bouquet garni
- 50g butter
- 2 leeks, sliced
- 2 tbsp plain flour
- grated zest 1 lemon
- large bunch parsley, chopped
- 3 tbsp crème fraîche
- 250g ready-made puff pastry
- beaten egg, or milk, to glaze

1 Put the chicken in a pan, which is large enough to take it snugly. Roughly chop the carrot, onion and celery and tuck around the chicken with the bouquet garni. Pour in enough water to come just over halfway up the chicken, then season with salt and pepper.

2 Bring to the boil, then reduce the heat, cover tightly and simmer gently for 1–1¼ hrs, until the chicken is well cooked. Carefully lift the chicken out onto a board lined with kitchen paper to absorb any stock that leaks out. Then strain the stock, discarding the veggies, and measure 500ml into a jug – any extra you can cool and freeze for another time.

3 Heat the oven to 200C/fan 180C/gas 6. Strip the meat from the chicken, discarding the skin and bones. Cut the meat into large chunks and put into a 1-litre pie dish.

4 Melt the butter in a pan, add the leeks and fry until starting to soften. Sift in the flour and cook for 1 min. Gradually stir in the stock, cooking until the sauce is smooth and glossy. Take off the heat and add lemon, parsley and crème fraîche. Season. Pour the sauce over the chicken and leave to cool.

5 Roll out the pastry and trim to 5cm larger than the pie dish. Brush the edge of the dish with water. Lay the pastry on the pie, tucking the edges under to make a double layer around the rim. Press the pastry edge to seal it. Roll out any trimmings to make leaves for the top. If you want to freeze this pie, make up the filling and cool it in the pie dish, then top with the pastry and freeze. Then all you have to do is defrost the pie overnight and bake it as usual. Brush the pastry with milk or egg and bake for 30–35 mins until the pastry is golden.

Nutrition per serving (6)
kcal 401 • fat 23g • saturates 10g • carbs 21g • sugars 2g • fibre 1g • protein 28g • salt 0.60g

Minced beef Wellington

Sunday lunch with a money-saving twist.

MODERATELY EASY ⏱ PREP 20 mins COOK 1 hr 20 mins ◷ SERVES 8

- 1kg minced beef
- 100g tomato ketchup
- 4 eggs
- 3 onions, finely chopped
- 3 garlic cloves, finely chopped
- small handful sage, chopped
- handful parsley, chopped
- 25g butter
- 200g mushrooms, finely chopped
- 500g pack puff pastry
- mash and veg to serve

1 Mix the beef with the ketchup, 3 eggs, seasoning and 100ml water in a table-top mixer for 5 mins – or squeeze and squelch with your hands in a bowl. Mix in the onions, half the garlic and herbs.
2 Heat oven to 200C/180C fan/gas 6. Press the meat into a sausage shape about 30cm x 10cm on a baking tray. Cook for 20 mins then remove and leave to cool.
3 Heat the butter in a frying pan over a high heat, add the mushrooms and cook for 3 mins. Add remaining garlic and cook for a further 2 mins, pouring off the excess water from the mushrooms.
4 Roll the pastry into a rectangle large enough to wrap up the beef. Beat the remaining egg with a little water and brush over the pastry.
5 Spread the mushroom mix into a meatloaf-size strip along the middle of the pastry. Sit the meat on top, then cut the pastry either side into strips from the meat outwards. Criss-cross these over the meat to enclose and tuck under the ends. Brush with more egg, then place on a tray and cook for about 40 mins, covering after 30 mins if going too brown. Can be frozen unbaked; wrap loosely until frozen, then rewrap tightly.

Nutrition per serving
kcal 640 • fat 45g • saturates 20g • carbs 27g • sugars 7g • fibre 2g • protein 33g • salt 1.42g

Chicken tikka masala

This takeaway favourite is freezer-friendly and quick to reheat, giving you the chance to get ahead and save money.

EASY · PREP 15 mins COOK 45 mins · MAKES 10 SERVINGS

- 4 tbsp vegetable oil
- 25g butter
- 4 onions, roughly chopped
- 6 tbsp chicken tikka masala curry paste
- 2 red peppers, deseeded and cut into chunks
- 8 boneless, skinless chicken breasts, cut into 2.5cm cubes
- 2 x 400g cans chopped tomatoes
- 4 tbsp tomato purée
- 2–3 tbsp mango chutney
- 150m double cream
- 150ml natural yogurt
- chopped coriander leaves to serve

1 Heat the oil and butter in a large, lidded casserole on the hob, then add the onions and a pinch of salt. Cook for 15–20 mins until soft and golden. Add the paste and peppers, then cook for 5 mins more to cook out the rawness of the spices.

2 Add the chicken and stir well to coat in the paste. Cook for 2 mins, then tip in the tomatoes, purée and 200ml water. Cover with a lid and gently simmer for 15 mins, stirring occasionally, until the chicken is cooked through.

3 Remove the lid, stir through the mango chutney, cream and yogurt, then gently warm through. Season, then set aside whatever you want to freeze. To safely freeze, cool the curry as quickly as possible, then freeze as soon as it's completely cooled. To avoid freezer burn, make sure all chicken pieces are well covered with sauce. This curry will freeze well for up to 3 months. Defrost overnight in the fridge. Once thoroughly defrosted, reheat gently to prevent yogurt from splitting. Make sure it's piping hot all the way through before serving. Scatter the rest with coriander leaves and serve with basmati rice and naan bread.

Nutrition per serving
kcal 345 · fat 19g · saturates 8g · carbs 13g · sugars 10g · fibre 3g · protein 31g · salt 1.04g

5-a-day Bolognese

Get all 5 of your 5-a-day with this spaghetti Bolognese. The veg in the sauce makes it ideal for kids and you can freeze any leftovers.

MORE EFFORT 🕐 PREP 20 mins COOK 1 hr 🕐 SERVES 2

- 1½ tbsp olive oil
- 150g beef mince
- 2 onions, finely chopped
- 2 leeks, finely sliced
- 1–2 garlic cloves, crushed
- 1 red pepper, chopped into small pieces
- 1 large courgette, chopped into small pieces
- 1 can chopped tomatoes
- 2 tbsp tomato purée
- 50ml chicken or beef stock
- ½ tsp dried oregano
- 150g spaghetti
- 25g Parmesan, finely grated
- a few basil leaves (optional)

1 Put ½ tbsp of the oil in a large saucepan over a medium-high heat, add the beef and fry until well browned. Tip out into a dish and put the pan back on the heat with the remaining oil. Turn the heat down and cook the onions and leeks for 8–10 mins or until they are very soft, then add the garlic, pepper and courgette. Fry until the veg is starting to char at the edges and any water that's been released has evaporated.

2 Tip the meat back into the pan and add the tomatoes, purée, stock and oregano. Stir everything together, cover and simmer over a low heat, stirring occasionally, for 35 mins. You can freeze the meat at this point.

3 Meanwhile cook the spaghetti following pack instructions, then towards the end of cooking, stir half the Parmesan into the Bolognese. Put a spoonful of the pasta water into the sauce to loosen it, if it looks too thick, then drain the spaghetti. Tip the pasta onto the sauce, toss everything together to coat and season well. Garnish with the remaining Parmesan and a few basil leaves.

Nutrition per serving
kcal 722 • fat 27g • saturates 9g • carbs 76g • sugars 26g • fibre 15g • protein 37g • salt 0.5g

Chicken & chorizo ragu

Serve this delicious chicken and chorizo ragu over rice or pasta as an easy midweek dinner for the family. You can freeze any leftovers for another day.

EASY ○ PREP 15 mins COOK 1 hr ○ SERVES 4

- 120g cooking chorizo, chopped
- 1 red onion, chopped
- 2 garlic cloves, grated
- 1 tsp hot smoked paprika
- 80g sundried tomatoes, roughly chopped
- 600g skinless and boneless chicken thighs
- 400g can chopped tomatoes
- 100ml chicken stock
- 1 lemon, juiced
- jacket potatoes, chopped parsley and soured cream to serve (optional)

1 Fry the chorizo over a medium heat in a large saucepan or flameproof casserole dish for 5 mins or until it releases its oil and starts to char at the edges. Add the onion and fry for 5 mins more or until soft. Tip in the garlic and cook for 2 mins before stirring in the paprika and sundried tomatoes. Add the chicken thighs and fry for 2 mins each side until they are well coated in the spices and beginning to brown.

2 Pour in the chopped tomatoes and stock, and turn the heat down. Cover and cook for 40 mins until the chicken is falling apart and the sauce is thick. Stir the lemon juice through. Will freeze; cool properly first and reheat thoroughly to serve. Serve by piling spoonfuls of the ragu into hot jacket potatoes with parsley sprinkled over and a dollop of soured cream, if you like.

Nutrition per serving
kcal 383 • fat 15g • saturates 5g • carbs 16g • sugars 14g • fibre 5g • protein 44g • salt 1.5g

Butternut squash & chickpea tagine

Make this tasty vegetarian tagine that kids will love as much as grown-ups. It's a great way to serve 4 of their 5-a-day and it's freezeable.

EASY ⏱ PREP 5 mins COOK 30 mins ⏳ SERVES 2 ADULTS AND 2 CHILDREN

- 1 tbsp oil
- 1 red onion, finely chopped
- 2 garlic cloves, crushed
- 1 tsp grated ginger
- ½ tsp ground cumin
- 1 tsp ground coriander
- 1 tsp cinnamon
- ¼ tsp mild chilli powder
- 500g bag frozen butternut squash chunks
- 2 carrots, cut into small dice
- 1 courgette, cut into small dice
- 2 x 400g cans chopped tomatoes
- 1 x 400g can chickpeas, drained
- cooked couscous or rice to serve

1 Heat the oil in a heavy-based pan, then slowly cook the onion for around 10 mins until starting to caramelise. Stir in the garlic, ginger and spices and cook for a further 2 mins. Add the vegetables and canned tomatoes and bring to a simmer.

2 Put the lid on and simmer for around 15 mins or until all the veg are tender. Stir in the chickpeas, heat through and serve with couscous or rice. Will freeze once made.

Nutrition per serving (4 average portions)
kcal 232 • fat 5g • saturates 1g • carbs 32g • sugars 17g • fibre 10g • protein 9g • salt 0.1g

Posh prawn & smoked salmon pasties

Give the traditional pasty a seasonal makeover by filling it with delicious prawns and smoked salmon – perfect for a summer picnic.

MORE EFFORT ⏱ PREP 40 mins plus chilling COOK 50 mins 🕐 MAKES 4

FOR THE FILLING
- 100g potatoes, cut into small cubes
- 200g smoked salmon, roughly chopped
- 1 lemon, zested
- 2 drops of Worcestershire sauce
- 50ml double cream
- 600g cooked and peeled prawns, roughly chopped
- 1 large dill sprig, roughly chopped
- 3 tbsp finely chopped sundried tomatoes
- large pinch of cayenne pepper

FOR THE PASTRY
- 350g strong white flour
- 25g cold butter, diced
- 50g cold lard, diced
- 1 egg yolk, beaten, for glazing

1 Simmer the potatoes in salted water for 8–10 mins or until just cooked, then drain and leave to cool. Tip all the filling ingredients into a bowl, mix well, season with a little salt and chill until needed.

2 To make the pastry, tip the flour, butter, lard and a pinch of salt into a bowl and work the fats into the pastry with your fingers until it makes a fine crumb. Bring 150ml of water to the boil and gradually stir into the bowl with a spatula or wooden spoon (you may not need all the water). Work the flour mixture together to form a ball, tip onto a work surface and knead the dough so it becomes smooth. Divide the dough into four balls, wrap in cling film and chill for 30 mins.

3 Heat oven to 180C/160C fan/gas 4. Remove a ball of dough from the fridge and roll out to a rough 18cm circle. Spoon a quarter of the filling into the middle, then draw up the edges and seal the pasty, making sure all the air has been pushed out. Crimp or fold the edges, then lay on a baking sheet. Repeat the process for the remaining three.

4 Brush the pasties with the beaten egg yolk and sprinkle with a tiny pinch of flaky salt. Bake for about 40 mins until golden. Remove from the oven and rest for at least 10 mins. Eat warm or leave to cool. Will freeze; wrap individually and defrost thoroughly.

Nutrition per pasty
kcal 808 • fat 32g • saturates 14g • carbs 76g • sugars 6g • fibre 5g • protein 51g • salt 3.6g

Luxe fish pie

Salmon and smoked haddock are perfect partners in this creamy, cheesy fish dish – freeze ahead and thaw for a make-ahead dinner party main.

EASY ⏱ PREP 45 mins COOK 1 hr 10 mins ⏳ SERVES 8

- 500g thick white fish fillets, such as cod or haddock, unskinned
- 500g thick salmon fillet, unskinned
- 300g smoked haddock (preferably undyed)
- 700ml full fat or semi-skimmed milk
- 1 medium onion, cut into thin wedges
- 2 bay leaves
- 75g butter
- 75g plain flour
- 140g young spinach leaves
- 3 tbsp white wine or vermouth (optional)
- ½ small pack dill, roughly chopped

FOR THE CHEESY TOPPING
- 1½kg potatoes (ideally Maris Piper), cut into even-sized pieces
- 50g butter
- 100g mature cheddar, coarsely grated
- 300ml tub half-fat crème fraîche

1 Place the fish fillets in a large, wide saucepan and pour over the milk. Add the onion wedges and bay leaves, tucking them in around the fish. Bring to a very gentle simmer, then cover with a lid and remove from the heat immediately. Leave to stand and infuse for 10 mins or until the fish is just cooked. Drain the fish in a colander over a large jug to reserve the infused milk, then tip the fish into a bowl. Set aside.

2 Meanwhile, make the topping. Put the potatoes in a large saucepan of cold water, bring to the boil, then simmer for 15 mins or until the potatoes are soft but not falling apart. Drain well, return to the pan and mash with the butter, half the cheese and the crème fraîche until smooth. Season to taste and set aside.

3 To finish the filling, melt the butter in a medium saucepan and stir in the flour. Cook for a few secs, then gradually add the infused milk, stirring over a medium heat for 3 mins until the sauce is smooth and thick. Stir in the spinach and wine or vermouth, if using, and cook for 2 mins more. Remove from the heat and stir in the dill. Season to taste.

4 Heat oven to 200C/180C fan/gas 6. Spoon a third of the sauce into the base of a 3-litre shallow rectangular dish. Scatter half the fish fillets over the sauce, breaking them into chunky pieces and discarding the skin, any stray bones, onion and bay leaves as you go. Pour over another third of the sauce, then top with more fish. Continue the layers once more, finishing with sauce.

5 Spoon the potato over the fish mixture, starting at the edges. Swirl the potato with the back of a spoon and sprinkle over the remaining cheese. Can be frozen at this point, defrost before cooking. Place the dish on a baking tray and bake in the centre of the oven for 45 mins or until the potato is golden and the filling is bubbling.

Nutrition per serving
kcal 652 • fat 32g • saturates 17g • carbs 45g • sugars 8g • fibre 4g • protein 43g • Salt 1.6g

Lamb masala meatball curry

This meaty one-pot has a mouthwateringly rich and spicy sauce, makes up 2 of your 5-a-day and is freezable in the unlikely event you have leftovers!

EASY ⏱ PREP 20 mins COOK 30 mins ⏲ SERVES 4

FOR THE MEATBALLS
- 1 tbsp fennel seed, toasted
- 2 garlic cloves, finely grated
- thumb-sized piece ginger, finely grated
- 2 green chillies, deseeded and finely chopped
- 1 onion, finely chopped
- 60g desiccated coconut
- 400g lamb mince

FOR THE CURRY SAUCE
- 1 tbsp olive oil
- 1 onion, finely chopped
- 1 tsp grated ginger
- 1 tbsp garam masala
- 1 tsp turmeric
- 400g can chopped tomatoes
- 1 tbsp coconut yogurt
- ½ small pack coriander, roughly chopped
- rice or naan to serve

1 Put all the meatball ingredients in a large bowl and use your hands to combine everything together. Roll into about 16 balls, cover and chill until needed.

2 Heat the oil in a large, deep frying pan over a gentle heat and fry the onion, ginger and spices for 10 mins until the onion is softened. Tip in the tomatoes and a splash of water, and bring to the boil over a high heat. Drop in the meatballs and reduce the heat. Cover and simmer for 15 mins or until the meatballs are cooked. Can be frozen for up to one month. Mix through the yogurt, scatter over the coriander and serve with rice or naan bread.

Nutrition per serving
kcal 408 • fat 28g • saturates 16g • carbs 12g • sugars 9g • fibre 5g • protein 23g • salt 0.2g

Chicken, kale & mushroom pot pie

A satisfying chicken and mushroom one-pot that makes a great family supper or freeze leftovers for another day.

EASY ⏱ PREP 10 mins COOK 40 mins ⏲ SERVES 4

- 1 tbsp olive oil
- 1 large onion, finely chopped
- 3 thyme sprigs, leaves picked
- 2 garlic cloves, crushed
- 350g chicken breasts, cut into small chunks
- 250g chestnut mushrooms, sliced
- 300ml chicken stock
- 100g crème fraîche
- 1 tbsp wholegrain mustard
- 100g kale
- 2 tsp cornflour, mixed with 1 tbsp cold water
- 375g pack puff pastry, rolled into a circle slightly bigger than your dish
- 1 egg yolk, to glaze

1 Heat ½ tbsp oil over a gentle heat in a flameproof casserole dish. Add the onion and cook for 5 mins until softening. Scatter over the thyme and garlic, and stir for 1 min. Turn up the heat and add the chicken, frying until golden but not fully cooked. Add the mushrooms and the remaining oil. Heat oven to 200C/180 fan/gas 6.

2 Add the stock, crème fraîche, mustard and kale, and season well. Add the cornflour mixture and stir until thickened a little.

3 Remove from the heat and cover with the puff pastry lid, pressing into the sides of the casserole dish. Slice a cross in the centre and glaze with the egg. To freeze, cool the filling before putting on the pastry top, glaze and then freeze. Bake for 30 mins until the pastry is puffed up and golden.

Nutrition per serving
kcal 673 • fat 41g • saturates 20g • carbs 40g • sugars 6g • fibre 5g • protein 34g • salt 1.4g

Twice-cooked sticky duck

This recipe for tender, juicy duck with a honey glaze is staggered and takes out all the stress of doing it on the day.

EASY ⏱ PREP 20 mins plus overnight chilling COOK 2 hrs 15 mins ◔ SERVES 6

FOR THE DUCK
- 1 strip pared orange zest
- 6 duck legs
- 6 garlic cloves, smashed
- thumb-sized piece ginger, sliced
- 1½ tsp Chinese five-spice powder
- 100ml dark soy sauce
- 1 tbsp oyster sauce
- 1 tbsp golden caster sugar
- 50ml Shaohsing rice wine

TO GLAZE
- 1 tbsp honey
- ½ tsp Chinese five-spice powder

TO SERVE
- halved and sliced cucumber, coriander leaves, sliced chilli, cooked rice

1 The day before eating, tip all the ingredients for the duck into a pan and just cover with water. Bring to the boil, then turn down the heat, cover and simmer gently for 1 hr 30 mins until the duck is really tender (or a slow cooker for 4 hrs would be ideal). Remove the duck from the liquid, leave to cool, then chill in the fridge, uncovered. Chill the liquid separately too. Can be done up to 3 days ahead and kept in the fridge, covered, or frozen for up to 3 months.

2 The next day, remove all the fat from the stock, pour 400ml into a pan and simmer down by a third, or until intensely flavoured. The remaining stock can be frozen and used another time to poach meat or poultry.

3 Heat oven to 220C/200C fan/gas 7. For the glaze, mix 1 tbsp of the reduced stock with the honey and five-spice. Put the duck legs on a baking tray, skin-side up, and roast in the oven for 25–30 mins until they are hot and the skin is lacquered. Can be cooled and frozen for up to 2 months.

4 Arrange some cucumber on a serving platter with the duck on the side, then scatter over the coriander. Add some sliced chilli to the simmered stock and serve on the side for spooning over the rice. Serve with steamed pak choi.

Nutrition per serving
kcal 381 • fat 19g • saturates 5g • carbs 4g • sugars 4g • fibre 0g • protein 46g • salt 1.3g

Spinach & ricotta cannelloni

Keep a few portions of this vegetarian classic in the freezer and you'll never be stuck for a satisfying supper.

EASY ⏱ PREP 50 mins COOK 1 hr ⏲ MAKES 10 SERVINGS

FOR THE SAUCE
- 3 tbsp olive oil
- 8 garlic cloves, crushed
- 3 tbsp caster sugar
- 2 tbsp red wine vinegar
- 4 x 400g cans chopped chopped tomatoes
- small bunch basil leaves

FOR THE TOPPING
- 2 x 250g tubs mascarpone
- 3 tbsp milk
- 85g Parmesan or vegetarian cheese, grated
- 2 x 125g balls mozzarella, sliced

FOR THE FILLING
- 1kg spinach
- 100g Parmesan or vegetarian cheese, grated
- 3 x 250g tubs ricotta
- large pinch grated nutmeg
- 400g dried cannelloni

1 First make the tomato sauce. Heat the oil in a large pan and fry the garlic for 1 min. Add the sugar, vinegar, tomatoes and some seasoning and simmer for 20 mins, stirring occasionally, until thick. Add the basil and divide the sauce between 2 or more shallow ovenproof dishes. Set aside. Make a sauce by beating the mascarpone with the milk until smooth, season, then set aside.

2 Put the spinach in a large colander and pour over a kettle of boiling water to wilt it (you may need to do this in batches). When cool enough to handle, squeeze out the excess water. Roughly chop the spinach and mix in a large bowl with 100g Parmesan and the ricotta. Season well with salt, pepper and the nutmeg.

3 Heat oven to 200C/180C fan/gas 6. Using a piping bag or plastic food bag with the corner snipped off, squeeze the filling into the cannelloni tubes. Lay the tubes, side by side, on top of the tomato sauce and spoon over the mascarpone sauce. Top with Parmesan and mozzarella. You can now freeze the cannelloni, uncooked, or you can cook it first and then freeze. Bake for 30–35 mins until golden and bubbling. Remove from the oven and let stand for 5 mins before serving.

Nutrition per serving
kcal 711 • fat 47g • saturates 27g • carbs 44g • sugars 15g • fibre 5g • protein 30g • salt 1.59g

Thai prawn, potato & vegetable curry

A fragrant Thai curry that can be prepared ahead and frozen for a future Friday night on the couch. If you are freezing this dish, you need to use full-fat coconut milk.

EASY 🕐 PREP 15 mins COOK 30 mins 🕑 SERVES 8

- 1 tbsp olive oil
- 4 tbsp Thai green curry paste
- 1 lemongrass stalk, outer layer removed, finely chopped
- 2 red peppers, cut into chunky strips
- 450g baby new potatoes, halved
- 2 x 400g cans coconut milk, see intro
- 300ml chicken stock
- 5 kaffir lime leaves, torn
- 1 bunch spring onions, sliced
- 225g frozen peas
- 600g raw king prawns
- 100g bag baby spinach
- 2 tbsp Thai fish sauce
- bunch coriander, leaves picked
- juice 1 lime, plus extra wedges, to serve

1 Heat oil in a large frying pan or wok. Fry the curry paste and lemongrass for 1 min, until fragrant. Tip in peppers and new potatoes, then stir them to coat in the paste. Cook for 1–2 mins. Pour in coconut milk, stock and kaffir lime leaves, then bring to the boil. Simmer and cook for 15 mins, until potatoes are just tender.

2 Add the remaining ingredients, but if you're freezing, don't add spinach or coriander yet, and cook until the prawns turn pink, about 4 mins. Serve, with some extra lime wedges, if you like. *Cool before freezing in containers.* Defrost in the fridge for 48 hrs or leave out at room temperature until fully defrosted, about 6–8 hrs. Once defrosted, reheat gently on the hob until piping hot, then stir in the spinach and coriander to wilt before serving.

Nutrition per serving
kcal 324 • fat 20g • saturates 15g • carbs 18g • sugars 7g • fibre 3g • protein 20g • Salt 1.97g

Hearty lamb stew

A classic one-pot is the easy answer to midweek cooking. Hearty, filling, warming and packed full of veggies.

EASY ⏱ PREP 10 mins COOK 1 hr 40 mins 🕐 SERVES 4

- 1 tbsp vegetable oil
- 500g cubed stewing lamb
- 1 onion, thickly sliced
- 2 carrots, thickly sliced
- 2 leeks, thickly sliced
- 400ml hot vegetable or chicken stock
- 1 tsp dried rosemary or 1 fresh sprig
- 400g cannellini beans, rinsed and drained
- crusty bread or boiled potatoes to serve (optional)

1 Heat the oil in a large casserole. Tip in the lamb and cook for 5 mins until any liquid has disappeared, then add the onion, carrots and leeks. Cook for 5 mins more, stirring often, until the veg is starting to soften.

2 Pour over the stock, add the rosemary, cover with a lid and cook over a low heat for 1 hr. Stir in the beans and cook for 30 mins more, topping up with water if necessary, until the lamb is tender and cooked through. Serve with some crusty bread or potatoes, if you like. Will freeze for up to 2 months; defrost and reheat gently before serving.

Nutrition per serving
kcal 397 • fat 20g • saturates 8g • carbs 19g • sugars 8g • fibre 6g • protein 38g • salt 1.15g

Sticky spiced lamb shanks

This hearty, slow-cooked lamb dish is perfect for 2 to share as the nights start drawing in.

EASY ⏱ PREP 15 mins COOK 3 hrs ⏲ SERVES 4

- 3 tbsp olive oil
- 4 lamb shanks
- 4 onions, sliced
- 6 garlic cloves, sliced
- 1 cinnamon stick
- 2 tbsp each cumin and coriander seeds, crushed
- pinch of chilli flakes
- 2 x 400g cans chopped tomatoes
- 1 litre chicken or vegetable stock
- 4 tbsp pomegranate molasses
- 8 dried apricots, chopped
- 8 dried figs, chopped
- handful coriander, chopped

1 Heat oven to 180C/160C fan/gas 4. Add 1 tbsp oil to a tight-lidded casserole (that will fit all the shanks) and brown the shanks for a couple of mins, turning as you go. Remove and set aside. Add the remaining oil and onions to the pan and cook for about 10 mins until soft. Add garlic and spices and cook for 4 mins more. Tip in the tomatoes and stock, then nestle the shanks back in on their sides. Bring to a boil, cover and put in the oven. Cook for 2 hrs: turn the shanks now and then.

2 Remove the lid and stir through the molasses, apricots and figs. Cook, uncovered, for 30 mins more or until the meat is falling away from the bone.

3 Remove the shanks from the dish and wrap in foil to keep warm. Put the dish back onto the heat and cook down the juices until thick and saucy. Season, then serve the shanks, scattered with coriander, alongside some rice. Will freeze for up to 2 months; reheat gently.

Nutrition per serving
kcal 1114 • fat 55g • saturates 23g • carbs 64g • sugars 52g • fibre 10g • protein 95g • salt 1.93g

Cardamom lamb hotpot

Indian spices merge with a traditional potato-topped lamb casserole to create this batch-friendly bake.

EASY ⏱ PREP 45 mins COOK 3 hrs 35 mins ⏲ SERVES 8

- 2 large onions, roughly chopped
- 6 garlic cloves
- 50g root ginger, roughly chopped
- 3 tbsp sunflower oil
- 30 cardamom pods, seeds removed and ground
- 2 tsp ground coriander
- 1kg lean diced lamb
- 700ml lamb stock
- 2 fresh red chillies, deseeded and chopped
- 3 tbsp tomato purée
- 100g creamed coconut (from a block), chopped
- 20 fresh curry leaves
- 2 aubergines, cubed
- 400g bag spinach

FOR THE POTATO TOPPING
- 1½kg large new potato
- 2 tbsp sunflower oil
- 3 tbsp tamarind paste
- ½ tsp turmeric
- 1 tsp cumin seeds
- 10 fresh curry leaves

1 Put the onion, garlic and ginger in a food processor and blend to a purée. Heat the oil in a large pan and fry the onion purée for 20 mins until starting to colour, stirring frequently. Add the cardamom and coriander, and fry a few mins more.

2 Stir in the lamb, fry until it starts to brown, then pour in the stock. Add the chilli, tomato purée, coconut and curry leaves, then cover and simmer for 1 hr. Add the aubergines and cook for 30 mins more until the lamb and aubergine are tender.

3 Meanwhile, make the potato topping. Boil the potatoes whole in their skins for 15–20 mins until just tender, then drain and cool. Also, wilt the spinach in a hot pan. Cool and squeeze in your hands to remove as much water as you can. Peel and thickly slice the potatoes, then toss with the oil, tamarind, turmeric, cumin seeds, curry leaves and some seasoning.

4 Stir the spinach into the curry and spoon into 1 extra-large or 2 regular-size ovenproof dishe(s). Pile the potatoes on top and lightly press down. The dish can now be frozen; reheat from frozen making sure the centre of the dish is piping hot before serving. If eating straight away, heat oven to 160C/180C fan/gas 4 and bake for 50 mins–1 hr (add 30–40 mins if using an extra-large dish). Serve with chutney and raita or an Indian salad made with chopped red onion, coriander, tomatoes, cucumber and lemon juice.

Nutrition per serving
kcal 578 • fat 28g • saturates 13g • carbs 43g • sugars 14g • fibre 7g • protein 38g • salt 0.5g

Braised beef with anchovy toasts

This slow-cooked dish makes a cheaper cut of beef skirt tender and melt-in-the-mouth. It's freezable too so great for a simple, budget dinner party.

EASY ⏲ PREP 30 mins COOK 2 hrs 15 mins ⏲ SERVES 6

- 3 tbsp olive oil
- 1 large onion, finely chopped
- 4 garlic cloves, finely chopped
- 3 bay leaves
- 750ml bottle red wine
- 500ml beef stock
- 2 tsp caster sugar
- 2 tbsp plain flour
- 2 tbsp tomato purée
- 1½kg piece lean beef skirt, cut into large chunks
- 6 anchovies in oil, chopped
- 400g shallots, peeled
- 500g Chantenay carrots, stalk ends trimmed
- 140g Kalamata olives

FOR THE ANCHOVY TOASTS
- 6 anchovies in oil
- 100g unsalted butter
- 3 tbsp finely chopped parsley, plus extra to serve
- 1 French stick sliced, to serve

1 Heat the oil in a large, heavy-based casserole dish and fry the onion for 5 mins. Stir in the garlic and bay leaves and fry for 5 mins more.
2 Pour in the wine, stock and sugar. Mix the flour with the tomato purée and 3 tbsp water. Tip into the wine mixture and stir continuously until thickened. Then add the meat and anchovies, cover and leave to simmer for 1 hr.
3 Stir in the shallots, carrots and olives. Cover and simmer for 1 hr more until everything is tender. Meanwhile, for the anchovy toasts, grind the anchovy fillets using a pestle and mortar until smooth (or very finely chop), then beat into the butter with the parsley and lots of black pepper. If freezing, spoon the stew into a container or freezer bag. Repeat with the anchovy butter. To defrost, put both in the fridge to thaw overnight, then reheat the stew in a pan.
4 To serve, grill the slices of French bread until lightly toasted, then spread with the anchovy butter. Serve on top of the beef stew and scatter with parsley.

Nutrition per serving
kcal 740 • fat 37g • saturates 15g • carbs 29g • sugars 14g • fibre 5g • protein 65g • salt 3.04g

Italian sausage & pasta pot

This soup is hearty and packed with flavour, making a simple yet satisfying freezable favourite.

EASY ⏱ PREP 10 mins COOK 25 mins 🕐 SERVES 4

- 1 tbsp olive oil
- 8 Italian sausages
- 2.8 litres hot chicken stock
- 400g penne pasta
- 2 carrots, thinly sliced
- 2 onions, thinly sliced
- 3 celery sticks, thinly sliced
- 140g green beans, cut into 5cm lengths
- handful flat-leaf parsley, chopped

1 Heat the oil in a large pan and fry the sausages until brown all over. Pour in the hot chicken stock and simmer with a lid on for 10 mins.

2 Add the pasta to the pan, mix well and bring to the boil. Stir in the carrots and onions, cook for 5 mins, then add the celery and beans, and cook for a further 4 mins. Check that the pasta is cooked – if not, cook for a few minutes longer. If you are planning to freeze this in batches, then cook the pasta until it is al dente and no more and reheat it gently. Finally, stir in chopped parsley, season, and serve in large bowls.

Nutrition per serving
kcal 772 • fat 25g • saturates 8g • carbs 90g • sugars 11g • fibre 9g • protein 53g • salt 3g

Pan-fried chicken with tomato & olive sauce

A rustic, Italian-inspired chicken recipe that's perfect for using up a glut of tomatoes.

EASY · PREP 10 mins COOK 25 mins · SERVES 2

- 2 tbsp olive oil
- 2 boneless, skinless chicken breasts
- 1 small onion, halved and very thinly sliced
- 2 garlic cloves, shredded
- 400g ripe tomatoes, finely chopped
- 1 tbsp balsamic vinegar
- 6 pimiento-stuffed green olives, thickly sliced
- 300ml chicken stock
- generous handful basil leaves

1 Heat the oil in a large non-stick frying pan, then season the chicken and fry, flattest-side down, for 4–5 mins. Turn the chicken over, add the onion and cook 4–5 mins more. Lift the chicken from the pan and set aside. Add the garlic to the pan, then continue cooking until the onions are soft.

2 Tip in the tomatoes with the balsamic vinegar, olives, stock, half the basil and seasoning, then simmer, stirring frequently, for 7–8 mins until pulpy. Return the chicken and any juices to the pan and gently simmer, covered, for 5 mins more, to cook the chicken through. Serve scattered with the rest of the basil. Will freeze for up to 2 months, defrost and then heat through gently until piping hot.

Nutrition per serving
kcal 353 · fat 17g · saturates 3g · carbs 11g · sugars 9g · fibre 4g · protein 41g · salt 2.15g

Chicken biryani bake

Keep this biryani bake in the freezer for an easy midweek health kick.

EASY ⏱ PREP 10 mins COOK 1 hr 15 mins ⏏ SERVES 8

- 1 tbsp olive oil
- 4 skinless chicken breasts, chopped into chunks
- 4 skinless, boneless chicken thighs, chopped into chunks
- 2 onions, sliced
- 4 tbsp curry paste (we used korma and tikka masala)
- 300g cauliflower, chopped into small florets
- 700ml chicken stock
- 400g can chopped tomatoes
- 400g can chickpeas, rinsed and drained
- 200g natural yogurt
- 300g spinach
- 400g basmati rice, cooked following pack instructions
- 5 tbsp flaked almond

1 Start by making the curry. Heat the oil in a large, deep frying pan. Season the chicken and fry until browned, then remove and set aside. Fry the onion in the rest of the oil for 10–12 mins until soft and starting to caramelise.

2 Add the paste and cauliflower, stirring to coat everything, then return the chicken. Pour in the stock, tomatoes and chickpeas and simmer everything for 30 mins until the cauliflower is nearly tender. There should be just enough liquid to cover everything, so add a splash more water or stock if you need to. Remove from the heat and stir in the yogurt.

3 Assemble the bake in either 1 large or 2 smaller, deep ovenproof dishes. Start with a third of the spinach leaves, season, then top with a third of the curry. Finish with a third of the rice then repeat twice more. Scatter on the almonds and either cool completely to freeze, or heat oven to 220C/200C fan/gas 7 and cook for 20–25 mins until the topping has crisped up and the dish is piping hot through. The biryani bake can be cooked from frozen, but the cauliflower will become quite soft. Cover with foil and bake at 180C/160C/ gas 4 for 1 hr 45 mins, before removing the foil and baking at 220C/200C/gas 7 for 30 mins more until piping hot through. Or defrost at room temp, then cook as above in the recipe, just adding an extra 10–15 mins to the cooking time.

Nutrition per serving
kcal 463 • fat 11g • saturates 2g • carbs 54g • sugars 7g • fibre 5g • protein 40g • salt 1.31g

Sali murghi

Cook up a chicken curry packed with spices and a bit of sweetness from apricots and jaggery, an unrefined cane sugar. Serve with 'sali' – potato matchsticks.

EASY ⏱ PREP 20 mins COOK 55 mins ⏳ SERVES 6-8

- 2½ tbsp ghee or vegetable oil
- 8 chicken thighs
- 1 cinnamon stick
- 5 green cardamom pods, bashed, seeds removed
- 1 tsp cumin seeds
- 2 onions, finely chopped
- 2 green chillies, roughly chopped
- 3 garlic cloves, roughly chopped
- 5cm piece ginger, roughly chopped
- 1 tsp ground coriander
- 1 tsp ground garam masala
- 1 tsp Kashmiri chilli powder
- ½ tsp turmeric
- 3 medium tomatoes, around 300g, finely chopped (or blitzed)
- 2 tbsp white wine vinegar
- 2 tsp jaggery (or soft brown sugar)
- 150g dried apricots (use the soft, ready-to-eat type)
- ½ small pack coriander, chopped

FOR THE SALI (OPTIONAL)
- 1 large potato, peeled and sliced into matchsticks
- vegetable oil, for frying

1 Melt 1 tbsp of the ghee in a pan and add the chicken, skin-side side down. Once the skin is golden and crisp (around 5 mins), remove from the pan and set aside (you may need to do this in batches). Melt the remaining ghee in the pan, add the cinnamon, cardamom and cumin seeds, and fry until fragrant – around 5 mins. Stir in the onions along with a big pinch of salt and fry for 5 mins until browning in places.

2 Blitz the green chilli with the garlic and ginger, add to the pan and cook for 2 more mins, then stir in the spices and cook for a few mins more, splashing in a little water to prevent the spices from sticking. Tip in the tomatoes.

3 Return the chicken to the pan, coating it with the curry base, then splash in the white wine vinegar followed by the jaggery. Add 100ml water, then cover and simmer for 30 mins. Remove the lid and stir in the apricots and coriander, then cook for 10–15 mins longer, until the gravy reduces. Will freeze at this point for up to 2 months; defrost and then heat through thoroughly.

4 To make the sali. Pat the potato matchsticks dry with kitchen paper. Pour vegetable oil into a small, deep saucepan until it's a few cm deep, and heat over a medium-high heat. Add a handful of the potato matchsticks at a time and fry for around a minute, until golden and crisp. Remove with a slotted spoon, drain on kitchen paper and season generously. Serve the curry with the sali piled on top.

Nutrition per serving (6)
kcal 385 • fat 23g • saturates 8g • carbs 18g • sugars 16g • fibre 5g • protein 24g • salt 0.3g

Next level chilli con carne

Reinvent this classic comfort food with our one-pan version that is enriched with peanut butter, espresso powder and dark chocolate. You won't look back.

MORE EFFORT ⏱ PREP 25 mins COOK 3 hrs 30 mins ◷ SERVES 8

- 2 dried ancho chillies
- 2 tsp black peppercorns
- 2 tbsp cumin seeds
- 2 tbsp coriander seeds
- 2 tsp smoked paprika
- 1 tbsp dried oregano
- 3 tbsp vegetable oil
- 1½kg braising steak, cut into 4cm cubes – meat from the brisket, short rib, blade or chuck steak are all good
- 2 onions, finely chopped
- 6 garlic cloves, minced
- 2 tbsp tomato purée
- 1 tbsp smooth peanut butter
- ½ tsp instant espresso powder
- 2 tbsp apple cider vinegar
- 1 litre beef or chicken stock
- 2 bay leaves
- small piece of cinnamon stick
- 2 tbsp semolina, polenta or Mexican masa flour
- 25g dark chocolate (70–80% cocoa solids)
- 400g can kidney beans, drained but not rinsed (optional)

1 Heat oven to 140C/120C fan/gas 1. Over a high heat, toast the whole chillies on all sides until you can smell them cooking, then remove and set aside. Keep the pan on the heat and toast the peppercorns, cumin seeds and coriander seeds until they just start to change colour, then grind to a powder using a pestle and mortar or spice grinder. Mix with the smoked paprika and oregano (this is a standard tex-mex seasoning), then set aside.

2 Return the casserole to the heat, add half the oil and heat until shimmering. Fry the beef in batches, adding more oil if you need to, until it's browned on all sides, then set aside. Fry the onions in the pan over a low heat for about 8 mins until soft and golden, then add the garlic and cook for 1 min more. Working fast, add the meat and juices, the spice mix, tomato purée, peanut butter and coffee to the pan and cook for 2–3 mins, stirring to coat the meat until everything is thick and gloopy, then pour in the vinegar and stock.

3 Add the toasted chillies back into the casserole, along with the bay leaves, cinnamon and some salt. Bring to a simmer and stir well, then cover with the lid and cook in the oven for 3 hrs, stirring occasionally, until the meat is very tender but not falling apart. Take the casserole out of the oven, put back on the stove and remove the lid. Simmer the sauce for 5 mins, then stir in the semolina flour and simmer for 2–3 mins more. Finely grate over the chocolate, stir through with the beans and simmer for a minute more to heat through. Fish out the chillies, then leave everything to rest for at least 15 mins. Bring the pan to the table. Serve with bowls of accompaniments. Freeze in batches in freezer bags; defrost and then reheat thoroughly until piping hot.

Nutrition per serving
kcal 463 • fat 24g • saturates 9g • carbs 12g • sugars 4g • fibre 6g • protein 46g • salt 0.6g

Saucy meatball & carrot bake with crispy feta crumbs

A moreish meatball recipe that you can divide into batches and freeze for later – a great way to use up a glut of carrots.

EASY ⏱ PREP 30 mins COOK 1 hr ⏲ SERVES 8

- 900g pork mince
- 140g breadcrumbs
- 1 tbsp caraway seeds
- 1 egg
- 4 tsp ground cumin
- 750g carrots, peeled and halved lengthways, or quartered if they're really big
- 4 tbsp olive oil, plus extra for frying
- 3 onions, whizzed to a paste in a food processor
- good chunk ginger, grated
- 680g bottle passata
- 2 x 400g cans chopped tomatoes
- 2 tbsp sugar
- 200g pack feta cheese, crumbled
- small pack parsley, chopped

1 Heat oven to 220C/200C fan/gas 7. Mix the pork, 50g of the breadcrumbs, caraway seeds, egg and half the cumin with 2 tsp salt and lots of pepper. Roll into about 30 meatballs and put into a large non-stick roasting tin. Put the carrots into another roasting tin. Split the oil between the 2, and gently toss to coat. Roast for 30–40 mins, shaking the tins halfway (and swapping between shelves if you need to), until golden and cooked through.

2 Meanwhile, fry the onion, ginger and remaining cumin in a drop more oil for a few mins in a large pan, stirring constantly. Stir in the passata, chopped tomatoes, sugar and some seasoning, then simmer for 15 mins.

3 Divide the meatballs and carrots between baking dishes or tins and spoon over the tomato sauce. Mix the remaining breadcrumbs with the feta, parsley and some seasoning. Set aside any portions for freezing now. To make sure that the topping doesn't go soggy, freeze the crumbs in separate freezer bags. Then once the dishes of meatballs (and the crumbs) have defrosted, assemble and bake as below. Sprinkle the feta crumbs over any portions to be cooked immediately.

4 To eat now, reduce the oven to 200C/180C fan/gas 6 and bake for 20 mins until the crumbs are golden and everything is piping hot. If frozen, defrost the portions, finish assembling and bake at 180C/160C fan/gas 4 for 30–50 mins until everything is piping hot and bubbling – the cooking time will depend a bit on the portion size you are baking.

Nutrition per serving
kcal 488 • fat 24g • saturates 8g • carbs 38g • sugars 19g • fibre 5g • protein 33g • salt 1.85g

Vegetable tagine with apricot quinoa

As ingredients like pomegranates and preserved lemons are more readily available now, this recipe shows how simple it is to incorporate their punchy flavours into dishes at home. This vegan recipe is a good source of iron and gives you all 5 of your 5-a-day!

EASY 🕐 PREP 30 mins COOK 45 mins 🕐 SERVES 4

FOR THE TAGINE
- 1 tsp coconut oil or olive oil
- 1 red onion, chopped
- 2 garlic cloves, crushed
- ½ butternut squash (500g), deseeded, peeled and chopped
- 1 large aubergine (500g), chopped into large chunks
- 2 red peppers, chopped
- 400g can chickpeas, drained
- 400g can chopped tomatoes
- 500ml vegan veg stock
- 1 tsp ground cinnamon
- 1 tsp ground cumin
- 2 tsp turmeric
- 2 tsp paprika
- small bunch coriander and mint, chopped
- pomegranate seeds

FOR THE APRICOT QUINOA
- 280g quinoa
- 80g dried apricots, chopped
- 20g toasted flaked almonds

FOR THE DRESSING
- 4 tbsp tahini
- 2 tsp preserved lemon, finely chopped, plus 2 tsp liquid from the jar
- 6 tbsp almond milk

1 Heat the oil in a large frying pan and fry the onion over a medium heat for 3 mins. Add the garlic and butternut squash, and cook for a further 7 mins.

2 Add the remaining vegetables and continue to fry for 3 mins before adding the chickpeas, tomatoes and stock, along with the spices and seasoning. Simmer for 30 mins, uncovered. To freeze, cool and transfer to freezer bags or containers.

3 Meanwhile, put 750ml water in a small saucepan, bring to a simmer, then add the quinoa and cook for 20 mins. When cooked, stir in the apricots and almonds, plus a pinch of salt.

4 To make the tahini dressing, whisk together all the ingredients in a small bowl. Season with a pinch of salt.

5 Serve the quinoa with the tagine, and drizzle the tahini dressing over the top. Scatter over some chopped coriander and mint and the pomegranate seeds to finish.

Nutrition per serving
kcal 650 · fat 20g · saturates 3g · carbs 80g · sugars 31g · fibre 23g · protein 25g · salt 0.5g

Roasted aubergine & tomato curry

Slightly sweet with added richness from the coconut milk, this simple vegan curry is a winner.

EASY ⏱ PREP 15 mins COOK 45 mins ⏳ SERVES 4

- 600g baby aubergines, sliced into rounds
- 3 tbsp olive oil
- 2 onions, finely sliced
- 2 garlic cloves, crushed
- 1 tsp garam masala
- 1 tsp turmeric
- 1 tsp ground coriander
- 400ml can chopped tomatoes
- 400ml can coconut milk
- pinch of sugar (optional)
- ½ small pack coriander, roughly chopped
- rice or chapatis to serve

1 Heat oven to 200C/180C fan/gas 6. Toss the aubergines in a roasting tin with 2 tbsp olive oil, season well and spread out. Roast for 20 mins or until dark golden and soft.

2 Heat the remaining oil in an ovenproof pan or flameproof casserole dish and cook the onions over a medium heat for 5–6 mins until softening. Stir in the garlic and spices, for a few mins until the spices release their aromas.

3 Tip in the tomatoes, coconut milk and roasted aubergines, and bring to a gentle simmer. Simmer for 20–25 mins, removing the lid for the final 5 mins to thicken the sauce. Add a little seasoning if you like, and a pinch of sugar if it needs it. Stir through most of the coriander. Serve over rice or with chapatis, scattering with the remaining coriander. Can be frozen for up to 1 month; defrost gently before heating through.

Nutrition per serving
kcal 331 • fat 26g • saturates 16g • carbs 15g • sugars 12g • fibre 7g • protein 5g • salt none

Beetroot & squash Wellingtons with kale pesto

These vegan Wellingtons can be made ahead and cooked from frozen – even meat-eaters will love them!

MORE EFFORT 🕐 PREP 40 mins plus at least 1 hr chilling COOK 1 hr 20 mins 🕐 SERVES 6

- 1 red onion, cut into 8 wedges
- 250g raw beetroot, peeled and cut into small chunks
- ½ butternut squash, peeled and cut into small chunks
- 4 fat garlic cloves, unpeeled
- 6 tbsp olive oil
- 1 tbsp picked thyme leaves, plus extra for sprinkling
- 1 tbsp sumac, plus extra for sprinkling
- 250g pouch ready-to-eat Puy lentils
- 180g pack whole cooked chestnuts, roughly chopped
- 100g kale
- ½ lemon, juiced
- 2 x 320g packs ready-rolled puff pastry suitable for vegans (we used Jus-Rol)
- 2 tbsp almond milk

1 Heat oven to 190C/170C fan/gas 5. Toss the onion, beetroot, squash and garlic in a roasting tin with 2 tbsp olive oil, the thyme leaves, sumac and some seasoning. Roast for 45 mins until the vegetables are tender but still retain their shape, then stir in the lentils and half the chestnuts. Squeeze the garlic cloves from their skins, reserve half and squash the other 2 into the lentil mixture. Leave the mixture to cool completely.

2 Bring a large pan of salted water to the boil, tip in the kale, cook for 1 min until wilted, then drain and run under cold water until cool. Squeeze all the water from the kale, then put it in the small bowl of a food processor along with the reserved garlic cloves, chestnuts, the lemon juice, olive oil and some seasoning. Blitz to a thick pesto, and season to taste.

3 On a lightly floured surface, unravel the sheets of puff pastry. Cut each sheet into 3 widthways, spread one-third of the kale pesto along one half of the pastry, then divide the roasted veg and lentils between the pastry rectangles, heaping the mixture on top of the pesto and leaving one side free of filling so that it is easier to roll. Brush all the borders with half the milk, fold over the ends, then carefully roll the pastry lengthways to completely encase the filling into a roll. Place on a baking tray lined with baking parchment and chill for at least 1 hr, or cover with cling film and leave overnight. If freezing, cover and freeze on a lined baking tray for up to 3 months.

4 To bake from chilled, heat oven to 190C/170C fan/gas 3 and line a baking tray with parchment.

5 Brush the top of each Wellington with a little milk and sprinkle with a little sumac, then bake for 30 mins from chilled or 45 mins from frozen until crisp and golden. Scatter over extra thyme and some flaky sea salt and serve.

Nutrition per serving
kcal 669 • fat 38g • saturates 15g • carbs 63g • sugars 8g • fibre 8g • protein 13g • salt 1.5g

Vegan shepherd's pie

A warming vegan supper with porcini mushrooms, leeks, carrots, butternut squash and plenty of herbs, topped with crispy potatoes – it's low calorie, low fat and perfect for when the nights draw in.

EASY ⏱ PREP 30 mins COOK 1 hr 20 mins (1 hr 45 mins if making large pies) ◔ SERVES 8 (MAKES 8 INDIVIDUAL OR 2 LARGE PIES)

- 1.2kg floury potatoes, such as Maris Piper or King Edward
- 50ml vegetable oil
- 30g dried porcini mushrooms, soaked in hot water for 15 mins, then drained (reserve the liquid)
- 2 large leeks, chopped
- 2 small onions, chopped
- 4 medium carrots (about 300g), cut into small cubes
- 1 vegan veg stock cube
- 3 garlic cloves, crushed
- 2 tbsp tomato purée
- 2 tsp smoked paprika
- 1 small butternut squash, peeled and cut into cubes
- ½ small pack marjoram or oregano, leaves picked and roughly chopped
- ½ small pack thyme, leaves picked
- ½ small pack sage, leaves picked and chopped
- 4 celery sticks, chopped
- 400g can chickpeas
- 300g frozen peas
- 300g frozen spinach
- 20ml olive oil
- small pack flat-leaf parsley, chopped
- tomato ketchup, to serve

1 Put the unpeeled potatoes in a large saucepan, cover with water, bring to the boil and simmer for 40 mins until the skins start to split. Drain and leave to cool a little.

2 Meanwhile, heat the vegetable oil in a large heavy-based sauté pan or flameproof casserole dish. Add the mushrooms, leeks, onions, carrots and the stock cube and cook gently for 5 mins, stirring every so often. If it starts to stick, reduce the heat and stir more frequently, scraping the bits from the bottom. The veg should be soft but not mushy.

3 Add the garlic, tomato purée, paprika, squash and herbs. Stir and turn the heat up a bit, cook for 3 mins, add the celery, then stir and cook for a few more mins. Tip in the chickpeas along with the water in the can and reserved mushroom stock. Add the peas and spinach and stir well. Cook for 5 mins, stirring occasionally, then season, turn off and set aside. There should still be plenty of liquid and the veg should be bright and a little firm.

4 Peel the potatoes and discard the skin. Mash 200g with a fork and stir into the veg. Break the rest of the potatoes into chunks, mix with the olive oil and parsley and season. Divide the filling into the pie dishes and top with the potatoes. Cool, wrap and freeze at this point if you like. Defrost and continue with the recipe when you are ready. Heat oven to 190C/170C fan/gas 5 and bake the pies for 40–45 mins, until the top is golden and the filling is heated through. If making individual pies, check after 20 mins. Best served with tomato ketchup – as all great shepherd's pies are.

Nutrition per serving
kcal 348 • fat 11g • saturates 1g • carbs 43g • sugars 10g • fibre 13g • protein 11g • salt 0.5g

Coconut & spinach kadala curry

This flavour-packed chickpea curry is a vegan main or side dish that provides 3 of your 5-a-day.

EASY ⏱ PREP 15 mins COOK 25 mins ⏲ SERVES 4

FOR THE PASTE
- 2 tbsp oil
- 1 onion, diced
- 1 tsp fresh or dried chilli, to taste
- 9 garlic cloves (approx 1 small bulb of garlic)
- thumb-sized piece ginger, peeled
- 1 tbsp ground coriander
- 2 tbsp ground cumin
- 1 tbsp garam masala
- 2 tbsp tomato purée

FOR THE CURRY
- 2 x 400g cans chickpeas, drained
- 400g can chopped tomatoes
- 100g creamed coconut
- ½ small pack coriander, chopped, plus extra to garnish
- 100g spinach

TO SERVE
- cooked rice and/or dhal

1 To make the paste, heat a little of the oil in a frying pan, add the onion and chilli, and cook until softened, about 8 mins. Meanwhile, in a food processor, roughly combine the garlic, ginger and remaining oil, then add the spices, tomato purée, ½ tsp salt and the fried onion. Blend to a smooth paste – add a drop of water or more oil, if needed.

2 Cook the paste in a medium saucepan for 2 mins over a medium-high heat, stirring occasionally so it doesn't stick. Tip in the chickpeas and chopped tomatoes, and simmer for 5 mins until reduced down. Add the coconut with a little water, cook for 5 mins more, then add the coriander and spinach, and cook until wilted. Garnish with extra coriander and serve with rice or dhal (or both). Will freeze for up to a month; defrost in the fridge before reheating gently.

Nutrition per serving
kcal 458 · fat 28g · saturates 16g · carbs 31g · sugars 9g · fibre 10g · protein 15g · salt 0.2g

Pumpkin curry with chickpeas & spinach

This is a fantastic vegetarian dinner party dish, it stands alone as a vegan main course and also makes a complex side dish to serve with spiced roast meat or fish.

EASY ⏱ PREP 20 mins COOK 20 mins ⏳ SERVES 4

- 1 tbsp sunflower oil
- 3 tbsp Thai yellow curry paste
- 2 onions, finely chopped
- 3 large stalks of lemongrass, bashed with the back of a knife
- 6 cardamom pods
- 1 tbsp mustard seeds
- 1 piece pumpkin or a small squash (about 1kg)
- 250ml vegetable stock
- 400ml can reduced-fat coconut milk
- 400g can chickpeas, drained and rinsed
- 2 limes
- large handful mint leaves
- naan bread to serve

1 Heat the oil in a sauté pan, then gently fry the curry paste with the onions, lemongrass, cardamom and mustard seeds for 2–3 mins until fragrant. Stir the pumpkin or squash into the pan and coat in the paste, then pour in the stock and coconut milk. Bring everything to a simmer, add the chickpeas, then cook for about 10 mins until the pumpkin is tender. The curry can now be cooled and frozen for up to 1 month.

2 Squeeze the juice of 1 lime into the curry, then cut the other lime into wedges to serve alongside. Just before serving, tear over the mint leaves, then bring to the table with the lime wedges and warm naan breads.

Nutrition per serving
kcal 293 • fat 18g • saturates 10g • carbs 26g • sugars 10g • fibre 7g • protein 9g • salt 1.32g

Indian winter soup

This warming winter soup is high in fibre, low in fat and can be frozen in batches for convenience.

EASY ⏱ PREP 15 mins COOK 30 mins 🕐 SERVES 4–6

- 100g pearl barley
- 2 tbsp vegetable oil
- ½ tsp brown mustard seeds
- 1 tsp cumin seeds
- 2 green chillies, deseeded and finely chopped
- 1 bay leaf
- 2 cloves
- 1 small cinnamon stick
- ½ tsp ground turmeric
- 1 large onion, chopped
- 2 garlic cloves, finely chopped
- 1 parsnip, cut into chunks
- 200g butternut squash, cut into chunks
- 200g sweet potato, cut into chunks
- 1 tsp paprika
- 1 tsp ground coriander
- 225g red lentils
- 2 tomatoes, chopped
- small bunch coriander, chopped
- 1 tsp grated ginger
- 1 tsp lemon juice

1 Rinse the pearl barley and cook following pack instructions. When it is tender, drain and set aside. Meanwhile, heat the oil in a deep, heavy-bottomed pan. Fry the mustard seeds, cumin seeds, chillies, bay leaf, cloves, cinnamon and turmeric until fragrant and the seeds start to crackle. Tip in the onion and garlic, then cook for 5–8 mins until soft.

2 Stir in the parsnip, butternut and sweet potato and mix thoroughly, making sure the vegetables are fully coated with the oil and spices. Sprinkle in the paprika, ground coriander and seasoning, and stir again.

3 Add the lentils, pearl barley, the tomatoes and 1.7 litres water. Bring to the boil, then turn down and simmer until the vegetables are tender. When the lentils are almost cooked, stir in the chopped coriander, ginger and lemon juice. Will freezer for up to a month; defrost in the fridge and reheat gently.

Nutrition per serving [6]
kcal 445 • fat 8g • saturates 1g • carbs 80g • sugars 13g • fibre 8g • protein 19g • salt 0.14g

Chickpeas with tomatoes & spinach

··

This vegan curry provides 2 of your 5-a-day and is great served with rice or naan bread for a filling meal.

EASY 🕐 PREP 10 mins COOK 25 mins 🕒 SERVES 4

- 1 tbsp vegetable oil
- 1 red onion, sliced
- 2 garlic cloves, chopped
- ½ finger-length piece fresh root ginger, shredded
- 2 mild red chillies, thinly sliced
- ½ tsp turmeric
- ¾ tsp garam masala
- 1 tsp ground cumin
- 4 tomatoes, chopped
- 2 tsp tomato purée
- 400g can chickpeas, rinsed and drained
- 200g pack baby spinach leaves
- rice or naan bread to serve

1 Heat the oil in a wok and fry the onion over a low heat until softened. Stir in the garlic, ginger and chillies and cook for a further 5 mins until the onions are golden and the garlic slightly toasted.

2 Add the turmeric, garam masala and cumin, stirring over a low heat for a few secs. Tip in the chopped tomatoes and add the tomato purée, then simmer for 5 mins.

3 Add the chickpeas to the pan with 300ml water (fill the can three-quarters full). Simmer for 10 mins before stirring in the spinach to wilt. Season and serve with rice or naan bread. Will freeze for up to a month; defrost in the fridge and reheat gently.

··

Nutrition per serving
kcal 145 • fat 6g • saturates none • carbs 17g • sugar 6g • fibre 5g • protein 7g • salt 0.56g

Mediterranean casserole

A Mediterranean one-pot stew with peppers, courgettes, lentils, sweet smoked paprika and thyme.

EASY ⏱ PREP 10 mins COOK 40 mins ⏲ SERVES 4

- 1 tbsp olive or rapeseed oil
- 1 onion, finely chopped
- 3 garlic cloves, sliced
- 1 tsp smoked paprika
- 1 tsp cumin
- 1 tbsp dried thyme
- 3 medium carrots, sliced (about 200g)
- 2 medium sticks celery, finely sliced (about 120g)
- 1 red pepper, chopped
- 1 yellow pepper, chopped
- 2 x 400g cans tomatoes or peeled cherry tomatoes
- 250ml vegetable stock cube (we used 1 Knorr vegetable stock pot)
- 2 courgettes, sliced thickly (about 300g)
- 2 sprigs fresh thyme
- 250g cooked lentils (we used Merchant Gourmet ready-to-eat Puy lentils)

1 Heat the oil in a large, heavy-based pan. Add the onion and cook gently for 5–10 mins until softened.
2 Add the garlic, spices, dried thyme, carrots, celery and peppers and cook for 5 minutes.
3 Add the tomatoes, stock, courgettes and fresh thyme and cook for 20–25 minutes.
4 Take out the thyme sprigs. Stir in the lentils and bring back to a simmer. Serve with wild and white basmati rice, mash or quinoa. Will freeze for up to a month; defrost in the fridge and reheat gently.

Nutrition per serving
kcal 216 • fat 5.1 g • saturates 0.7g • carbs 31g • sugars 16.1g • protein 12.3g • fibre 9.8g • salt 1.6 g

Sweetcorn & sweet potato burgers

Bulk out your burgers with polenta, then spice with cumin, chilli and coriander. Suitable for ovens and barbecues.

PREP 20 mins plus chilling COOK 1 hr 10 mins MAKES 10

- 6 large sweet potatoes (about 1.5kg)
- 2 tsp oil, plus extra for the trays
- 2 red onions, finely chopped
- 2 red chillies, finely chopped (deseeded if you like)
- 1 tbsp ground cumin
- 1 tbsp ground coriander
- 340g can sweetcorn, drained
- small bunch coriander, chopped
- 200g polenta
- buns, salsa, onion and salad leaves to serve

1 Heat oven to 200C/180C fan/gas 6. Pierce the potato skins and place on a baking tray. Bake for 45 mins until really soft. Remove from the oven and leave to cool. Meanwhile, heat the oil in a small pan, add the onions and chillies, and cook for 8–10 mins until soft. Leave to cool.

2 Peel the potatoes and add the flesh to a bowl with the chilli onions. Mash together with the spices until smooth. Using your hands, mix in the sweetcorn, coriander, half the polenta and some seasoning. Shape the mixture into 10 burgers; it will be quite soft. Carefully dip each one into the remaining polenta; dust off any excess. Place the burgers on oiled baking trays and chill for at least 30 mins. You can wrap and freeze the burgers at this stage.

3 Light the barbecue. When the flames have died down, place a large, well-oiled non-stick frying pan or sturdy baking tray on top of the bars. Cook the burgers in the pan or on the tray for 10 mins each side until nicely browned. Alternatively, heat oven to 220C/200C fan/gas 7 and cook on the oiled baking trays for 15 mins. Serve in buns with a dollop of salsa, some onion and salad leaves.

Nutrition per burger
kcal 252 • fat 2g • saturates none • carbs 54g • sugars 12g • fibre 6g • protein 5g • salt 0.4g

Choc-cherry fudge torte with cherry sorbet

You'd never guess that this divine, squidgy chocolate cake is vegan, nut-free and gluten-free.

A LITTLE EFFORT ⏲ PREP 25 mins plus soaking COOK 45 mins ⌛ CUTS INTO 10 SLICES

- 100g dried sour cherries
- 5 tbsp brandy
- 300g gluten- and wheat-free plain flour (we used Doves Farm)
- 85g cocoa, plus extra for dusting
- 200g light soft brown sugar
- 1 tsp each gluten-free baking powder and bicarbonate of soda
- 1 tsp xanthan gum
- 150ml sunflower oil
- 350ml rice milk (preferably unsweetened)
- 150ml agave syrup
- a little icing sugar, for dusting

FOR THE SORBET
- 2 x 600g jars cherry compote
- 200g caster sugar

1 For the sorbet, whizz the compote with the sugar until smooth-ish, then tip into a freezerproof container. Freeze until solid.
2 Mix the cherries and the brandy and leave to soak for a few hrs.
3 Heat oven to 160C/140C fan/gas 3. Line the base of a round, 20cm loose-bottomed tin with baking parchment. Mix the flour, cocoa, brown sugar, baking powder, bicarb and xanthan gum in a big bowl. Whisk the oil, rice milk and agave syrup, then add to the dry ingredients and stir in with a wooden spoon. Add the cherries and any brandy, then scrape into the tin. Bake for 35–45 mins until crisp on top but fudgy in the centre. Cool in the tin. To freeze, wrap the tin in cling film first, defrost in the tin and warm through in a hot oven.
4 Carefully lift the torte onto a serving plate. Dust with cocoa and icing sugar, and serve with the cherry sorbet.

Nutrition per slice
kcal 582 • fat 18g • saturates 3g • carbs 101g • sugars 71g • fibre 3g • protein 4g • salt 0.7g

Quinoa stew with squash, prunes & pomegranate

Get a dose of iron and protein with this healthy, vegan casserole that's full of texture and flavour.

PREP 15 mins COOK 40 mins SERVES 4

- 1 small butternut squash, deseeded and cubed
- 2 tbsp olive oil
- 1 large onion, thinly sliced
- 1 garlic clove, chopped
- 1 tbsp finely chopped ginger
- 1 tsp ras el hanout or Middle Eastern spice mix
- 200g quinoa
- 5 prunes, roughly chopped
- juice 1 lemon
- 600ml vegetable stock
- seeds from 1 pomegranate
- small handful mint leaves

1 Heat oven to 200C/180C fan/gas 6. Put the squash on a baking tray and toss with 1 tbsp of the oil. Season well and roast for 30–35 mins or until soft.
2 Meanwhile, heat the remaining oil in a big saucepan. Add the onion, garlic and ginger, season and cook for 10 mins. Add the spice and quinoa, and cook for another couple of mins. Add the prunes, lemon juice and stock, bring to the boil, then cover and simmer for 25 mins.
3 When everything is tender, stir the squash through the stew. Will freeze at this point; defrost in the fridge and reheat carefully. Spoon into bowls and scatter with pomegranate seeds and mint to serve.

Nutrition per serving
kcal 318 • fat 9g • saturates 1g • carbs 50g • sugars 20g • fibre 6g • protein 11g • salt 0.5g

Sweet potato & black bean chilli with zesty quinoa

This includes a little yeast extract, which helps to boost vitamin B12 intake. The quinoa and pumpkin seed mix will give you an added hit of protein. Serve with brown or white rice for a satisfying meal. Any leftovers will freeze well for up to 2 months.

EASY ⏱ PREP 25 mins COOK 45 mins ⏲ SERVES 3

- 1 tbsp rapeseed oil
- 2 sweet potatoes, peeled and cut into 2.5cm cubes
- 1 onion, chopped
- 2 fat garlic cloves, crushed
- 1 red chilli, seeds removed if you don't like it too hot, and finely chopped
- small bunch coriander, stalks finely chopped, leaves roughly chopped (keep them separate)
- 2 tsp each ground coriander, cumin and smoked paprika
- 2 tsp chipotle paste (ensure you use a gluten-free variety)
- 1 heaped tsp vegan-friendly yeast extract
- 2 x 400g cans chopped tomatoes
- 400g can black beans
- 140g quinoa, cooked according to pack instructions, or 250g pack ready-cooked quinoa
- zest and juice 1 lime
- 1 tbsp pumpkin seeds
- 1 ripe avocado, peeled and cubed

1 Heat oven to 180C/160C fan/gas 4. Toss the potatoes with half the oil and some seasoning on a baking tray. Bake for 30 mins, tossing halfway through cooking, until tender. Meanwhile, heat the remaining oil in a pan, add the onion and cook for 5 mins until soft, then add the garlic, chilli and coriander stalks. Cook everything for a further 2–3 mins, stirring to prevent the garlic from burning. Sprinkle in the spices, stirring for 1 min more, until aromatic. Stir in the chipotle paste, yeast extract, tomatoes and half a can of water, swirling it around the tin to wash out all the bits of tomato. Simmer the sauce, uncovered, while the sweet potato is cooking, adding a splash more water if it looks too dry.

2 Add the sweet potato, black beans and seasoning to the chilli. Bubble for 5 mins, then taste and adjust the seasoning with a squeeze of lime and a sprinkle of sugar if it needs it. Will freeze at this point for up to 2 months.

3 To serve, stir the lime zest, a squeeze of lime juice, the coriander leaves and the pumpkin seeds into the quinoa. Toss the avocado in the remaining lime juice as soon as you've cut it – this will prevent it turning brown. To serve, divide the quinoa among plates or bowls, top with the chilli and a pile of avocado.

Nutrition per serving
kcal 551 • fat 20g • saturates 3g • carbs 73g • sugars 18g • fibre 15g • protein 22g • salt 1.7g

Vegan cherry & almond brownies

Deeply rich and decadent, this dairy- and egg-free chocolate bake makes for an indulgent vegan treat.

EASY ⏱ PREP 20 mins COOK 45 mins ◔ MAKES 12

- 80g vegan margarine, plus extra for greasing
- 2 tbsp ground flaxseed
- 120g dark chocolate
- ½ tsp coffee granules
- 125g self-raising flour
- 70g ground almonds
- 50g cocoa powder
- ¼ tsp baking powder
- 250g golden caster sugar
- 1½ tsp vanilla extract
- 70g glacé cherries (rinsed and halved)

1 Heat oven to 170C/150C fan/gas 3½. Grease and line a 20cm square tin with baking parchment. Combine the flaxseed with 6 tbsp water and set aside for at least 5 mins.

2 In a saucepan, melt the chocolate, coffee and margarine with 60ml water on a low heat. Allow to cool slightly.

3 Put the flour, almonds, cocoa, baking powder and ¼ tsp salt in a bowl and stir to remove any lumps. Using a hand whisk, mix the sugar into the melted chocolate mixture, and beat well until smooth and glossy, ensuring all the sugar is well dissolved. Stir in the flaxseed mixture and vanilla extract, the cherries and then the flour mixture. It will now be very thick.

4 Stir until combined and spoon into the prepared tin. Bake for 35–45 mins until a skewer inserted in the middle comes out clean with moist crumbs. Allow to cool in the tin completely, then cut into squares. Store in an airtight container and eat within 3 days or wrap individually and freeze.

Nutrition per brownie
kcal 296 • fat 15g • saturates 5g • carbs 36g • sugars 27g • fibre 3g • protein 4g • salt 0.2g

Falafel burgers

Whizz up chickpeas with garlic, spices and herbs to make delicious vegetarian patties for lunch or dinner.

EASY 🕐 PREP 10 mins COOK 10 mins 🕐 SERVES 4

- 250g chickpeas from a can
- 1 medium onion, finely chopped
- 2 garlic cloves, crushed
- 2 tsp ground coriander
- 2 tsp ground cumin
- small pack flat-leaf parsley, chopped
- 2 rounded tbsp plain flour
- 2 tbsp vegetable oil
- 100g houmous
- 4 burger buns, cut in half
- watercress, to serve

1 Drain, rinse and dry the chickpeas thoroughly, then tip into the bowl of a food processor. Pulse until lightly broken up into coarse crumbs.
2 Add the onion, garlic, spices, parsley, flour and some seasoning, and continue to pulse until combined. Using your hands, gently form the mixture into 4 patties about 10cm in diameter and 2cm thick.
3 In a large pan, heat the oil and fry the falafels on each side for 2–3 mins or until golden (you may need to do this in batches). Will freeze at this point for up to 2 months; defrost thoroughly and warm through in a hot oven. Lightly griddle the burger buns on the cut side in a griddle pan, or toast under the grill.
4 Spread one side of each bun with houmous, top with a falafel burger, add a handful of watercress, then pop the remaining bun half on top.

Nutrition per serving
kcal 476 • fat 15g • saturates 2g • carbs 63g • sugars 5g • fibre 7g • protein 17g • salt 2.0g

Spiced aubergine bake

Aubergine is a brilliant, meaty vegetable that can really make a meal. It is especially divine in curries, where it holds its own against the strong spices and herbs. If you want to bulk out this full-of-flavour vegan dish even more, simply add a can of drained chickpeas in with the aubergines.

EASY 🕒 PREP 15 mins COOK 45 mins 🕒 SERVES 4-6

- 4 aubergines, cut into 5mm-1cm slices
- 3 tbsp vegetable oil
- 2 tbsp coconut oil
- 2 large onions, chopped
- 3 garlic cloves, crushed
- 1 tbsp black mustard seeds
- ½ tbsp fenugreek seeds
- 1 tbsp garam masala
- ¼ tsp hot chilli powder
- 1 cinnamon stick
- 1 tsp ground cumin
- 1 tsp ground coriander
- 2 x 400g cans chopped tomatoes
- 200ml coconut milk
- sugar, to taste
- 2 tbsp flaked almonds
- small bunch coriander, roughly chopped (optional)

1 Heat oven to 220C/200C fan/gas 7. Generously brush each aubergine slice with vegetable oil and place in a single layer on a baking tray, or two if they don't fit on one. Cook on the low shelves for 10 mins, then turn over and cook for a further 5–10 mins until they are golden. Reduce the oven to 180C/160C fan/gas 4.

2 Heat the coconut oil in a large, heavy-based frying pan and add the onions. Cover and sweat on a low heat for about 5 mins until softened. Add the garlic, mustard seeds, fenugreek seeds, garam masala, chilli powder, cinnamon stick, cumin and ground coriander. Cook for a few secs until it starts to smell beautiful and aromatic.

3 Pour the chopped tomatoes and coconut milk into the spiced onions and stir well. Check the seasoning and add a little sugar, salt or pepper to taste.

4 Spoon a third of the tomato sauce on the bottom of a 2-litre ovenproof dish. Layer with half the aubergine slices. Spoon over a further third of tomato sauce, then the remaining aubergine slices, and finish with the rest of the sauce. Sprinkle over the flaked almonds and coriander (if using), reserving some to serve, and bake for 25–30 mins. Can be frozen baked or unbaked; reheat or cook once defrosted. Serve garnished with more coriander.

Nutrition per serving (6)
kcal 318 • fat 20g • saturates 9g • carbs 19g • sugars 15g • fibre 12g • protein 8g • salt 0.2g

Vegan carrot cake

Give free-from baking a go with this easy vegan sandwich cake – an indulgent carrot cake with coconut and cashew icing that everyone will want another slice of.

EASY · PREP 35 mins COOK 25 mins · SERVES 12–15

FOR THE ICING
- 4 sachets (200g) creamed coconut
- 1 tbsp lemon juice
- 2 tbsp cashew nut butter
- 50g icing sugar
- 60ml oat milk

FOR THE CAKE
- 250ml jar coconut oil, melted
- 300g light brown sugar
- 1½ tsp vanilla essence
- 210ml dairy free milk, we used oat milk
- 420g plain flour
- 1½ tsp baking powder
- 1½ tsp bicarbonate of soda
- 1 tsp cinnamon, plus extra cinnamon to decorate
- 1 tsp ginger
- 1 tsp ground nutmeg
- 1 orange, zest only
- 4 medium carrots, grated (you want 270g grated weight)
- 75g chopped walnuts, plus extra to decorate
- edible flowers (optional)

1 Start by making the icing first. Mash the coconut cream with 2 tbsp hot water and the lemon juice until smooth. Add the cashew butter then whisk in the icing sugar followed by the oat milk. Continue to whisk until fully combined, set aside in the fridge until needed.

2 Heat the oven to 180C/160C fan/gas mark 4. Grease 2 x 20cm cake tins with a little of the melted coconut oil and line the bases with baking parchment.

3 Whisk together the oil and sugar, then add the vanilla and milk. Combine the flour, baking powder, bicarbonate of soda, spices and orange zest in a separate bowl. Add these to the wet mixture and stir well. Finally stir in the carrot and the nuts. Divide the mixture between the prepared tins and bake for 25–30 mins until a skewer inserted into the middle of the cake comes out cleanly. Cool in the tin for 5 mins before transferring to a wire rack to cool completely.

4 Sandwich the cakes together with half the icing then cover the top with the remaining icing (add a splash of oat milk if the icing feels too firm). Will freeze whole or as 2 separate sponges. Scatter over the nuts and dust the cake with a little cinnamon and decorate with edible flowers.

Nutrition per serving (15)
kcal 501 · fat 31g · saturates 23g · carbs 49g · sugars 26g · fibre 2g · protein 5g · salt 0.45g

Really easy roasted red pepper sauce

This red pepper sauce is so handy to have bagged in the freezer. The recipe makes enough for two meals – use as a base for baked gnocchi or pasta.

EASY ⏱ PREP 10 mins COOK 1 hr ⏰ SERVES 8 (OR 2 MEALS FOR 4)

- 4 red peppers (or a mix of red, orange and yellow), cut into chunks
- 2 onions, roughly chopped
- 2 garlic cloves (skin left on)
- 2 tbsp olive oil
- 2 x 400g cans peeled plum tomatoes
- 2 tsp red wine vinegar
- 1 tsp light soft brown sugar

1 Heat oven to 190C/170C fan/gas 5. Toss the peppers and onions with the garlic and olive oil, and spread out in a roasting tin. Roast for 40 mins, then add the tomatoes, red wine vinegar and sugar, and roast for another 20 mins. Tip into a food processor and blend until smooth. Season to taste. Bag up into portions to freeze.

Nutrition per serving
kcal 83 • fat 3g • saturates 1g • carbs 10g • sugars 9g • fibre 3g • protein 2g • salt 0g

Sweet potato & coconut curry

Prep your veggies and let the slow cooker do the work with our filling sweet potato curry.

MORE EFFORT ⏰ PREP 20 mins COOK 6 hrs 30 mins 🕐 SERVES 6

- 4 tbsp olive oil
- 2 large onions, halved and sliced
- 3 garlic cloves, crushed
- thumb-sized piece root ginger, peeled
- 1 tsp paprika
- ½ tsp cayenne
- 2 red chillies, deseeded and sliced
- 2 red peppers, deseeded and sliced
- 250g red cabbage, shredded
- 1kg sweet potatoes, peeled and chopped into chunks
- 300g passata
- 400ml coconut milk
- 2 tbsp peanut butter

TO SERVE
- small bunch fresh coriander, chopped
- cooked couscous

1 Heat 1 tbsp olive oil in a large non-stick frying pan and add the onion. Fry gently for 10 mins until soft then add the garlic and grate the ginger straight into the pan. Stir in the paprika and the cayenne and cook for another minute then tip into the slow cooker.

2 Return the pan to the heat and add another 1 tbsp oil along with the chilli, red pepper and shredded cabbage. Cook for 4–5 mins then tip into the slow cooker.

3 Use the remaining oil to fry the sweet potatoes, you may have to do this in 2 or 3 batches depending on the size of your pan. Cook the sweet potatoes for around 5 mins or just until they start to pick up some colour at the edges then put them in the slow cooker too.

4 Pour the passata and the coconut milk over the sweet potatoes, stir to mix everything together, cover the slow cooker with a lid and cook for 6-8 hrs or until the sweet potatoes are tender.

5 Stir the peanut butter through the curry, season well with salt and pepper and serve with couscous and chopped coriander scattered over the top. Will freeze for up to 2 months.

Nutrition per serving
kcal 434 • fat 22g • saturates 12g • carbs 47g • sugars 25g • fibre 10g • protein 6g • salt 0.2g

Butternut, chestnut & lentil cake

This stunning cake is a modern take on the classic nut roast, and the ideal vegan centrepiece, accompanied by all the usual trimmings.

A CHALLENGE 🕐 PREP 40 mins COOK 1 hr 45 mins 🕐 SERVES 8

- 1 large butternut squash, peeled with a veg peeler
- 3 tbsp sunflower oil, plus extra for greasing
- 3 onions, chopped
- 15g pack of sage, 12 leaves reserved, rest finely chopped
- 2 sprigs rosemary, leaves stripped and chopped, plus a few springs to serve
- 3 garlic cloves, crushed
- 1 tsp ground mace
- 2 tbsp ground chia seeds or linseeds (flaxseeds)
- 2 x 200g packs cooked chestnuts
- 2 x 400g cans brown lentils, rinsed and drained
- 200g wholemeal vegan breadcrumbs
- 3 tbsp rapeseed oil

1 Heat oven to 200C/180C fan/gas 6. Using a knife, cut a few 1cm thick ring-slices from the bulbous end of the squash, and some small slices from the top end. Dice the rest into 1-2cm chunks and toss with 1 tbsp of oil on a baking parchment-lined tray. Roast for 20–30 mins until golden.

2 Line the base of a deep, round, 25cm tin with baking parchment. Brush the new base and sides with oil, then arrange the rings in the base. You want to get in as many as you can, overlapping a bit like the Olympic rings. Snuggle in as many flat as you can, then sit overlapping ones on top, cutting out bits so they'll sit flat too. Any leftover trimmings, put in a microwave-proof bowl with a splash of water, cover with cling film and microwave on High at 2 min intervals until tender – around 5–6 minutes.

3 In a pan, soften the onion in the last 2 tbsp of oil over a very low heat so it doesn't brown. Stir in the chopped sage, half the rosemary and the garlic and mace, and cook for a few mins until fragrant. Mix the chia seeds with 4 tbsp of water, and set aside with the cooling onions until gluey.

4 Roughly chop half the chestnuts. Put the other half in a food processor with half the lentils, the microwaved squash and one-third of the roasted squash. Pulse to a mash and tip in a bowl with the onion, breadcrumbs, seeds and 1 tsp salt. Mash everything well, then gently stir in the chestnuts, whole lentils and squash chunks. Press this over the rings in the tin. Level off, making sure it's packed; cover with foil.

5 Heat the oven to 180C/160C fan/gas 4. Put the cake (still foil covered) on a middle shelf and bake for 1 hr. Will freeze for up to 2 months; cool first and wrap well.

6 To serve, heat the rapeseed oil in a pan and sizzle the sage leaves and rosemary for 1 min. Loosen around the cake with a knife, then sit a plate inverted on top, and flip to turn out the cake. Spoon over the herby oil and serve.

Nutrition per serving
kcal 316 • fat 11g • saturates 1g • carbs 42g • sugars 8g • fibre 7g • protein 8g • salt 0.3g

Lentil ragu with courgetti

A healthy tomato 'pasta' dish that makes full use of your spiralizer. This vegan-friendly supper is 5 of your 5-a-day and will fill you to the brim.

EASY ⊙ PREP 15 mins COOK 40 mins ⊙ SERVES 4–6

- 2 tbsp rapeseed oil, plus 1 tsp
- 3 celery sticks, chopped
- 2 carrots, chopped
- 4 garlic cloves, chopped
- 2 onions, finely chopped
- 140g button mushrooms from a 280g pack, quartered
- 500g pack dried red lentils
- 500g pack passata
- 1 litre reduced-salt vegetable bouillon (we used Marigold)
- 1 tsp dried oregano
- 2 tbsp balsamic vinegar
- 1–2 large courgettes, cut into noodles with a spiraliser, julienne peeler or knife

1 Heat the 2 tbsp oil in a large sauté pan. Add the celery, carrots, garlic and onions, and fry for 4–5 mins over a high heat to soften and start to colour. Add the mushrooms and fry for 2 mins more.

2 Stir in the lentils, passata, bouillon, oregano and balsamic vinegar. Cover the pan and leave to simmer for 30 mins until the lentils are tender and pulpy. Check occasionally and stir to make sure the mixture isn't sticking to the bottom of the pan; if it does, add a drop of water.

3 To serve, heat the remaining oil in a separate frying pan, add the courgette and stir-fry briefly to soften and warm through. Serve half the ragu with the courgetti and chill the rest to eat on another day. Can be frozen for up to 3 months.

Nutrition per serving (4)
kcal 578 • fat 7g • saturates 1g • carbs 87g • sugars 19g • fibre 14g • protein 35g • salt 0.2g

Kidney bean curry

This recipe comes to the rescue when there's nothing in the fridge or you simply want something cheap, delicious and filling.

EASY ⏱ PREP 5 mins COOK 30 mins ◔ SERVES 2

- 1 tbsp vegetable oil
- 1 onion, finely chopped
- 2 garlic cloves, finely chopped
- thumb-sized piece of ginger, peeled and finely chopped
- 1 small pack coriander, stalks finely chopped, leaves roughly shredded
- 1 tsp ground cumin
- 1 tsp ground paprika
- 2 tsp garam masala
- 400g can chopped tomatoes
- 400g can kidney beans, in water
- cooked basmati rice, to serve

1 Heat the oil in a large frying pan over a low-medium heat. Add the onion and a pinch of salt and cook slowly, stirring occasionally, until softened and just starting to colour. Add the garlic, ginger and coriander stalks and cook for a further 2 mins, until fragrant.

2 Add the spices to the pan and cook for another 1 min, by which point everything should smell aromatic. Tip in the chopped tomatoes and kidney beans in their water, then bring to the boil.

3 Turn down the heat and simmer for 15 mins until the curry is nice and thick. The curry will freeze for up to 2 months. Season to taste, then serve with the basmati rice and the coriander leaves.

Nutrition per serving
kcal 282 • fat 8g • saturates 1g • carbs 33g • sugars 13g • fibre 14g • protein 13g • salt 0.1g

Vegan Yorkshire puddings

A Sunday dinner staple that you can now enjoy even if you're vegan. With only 5 ingredients and that characteristic puff, these modified Yorkies are sure to be a hit.

EASY ⏱ PREP 5 mins plus 1 hr resting COOK 30 mins ◷ MAKES 8

- 225g self-raising flour
- ½ tsp baking powder
- 300ml unsweetened soya milk
- 100ml warm water
- 8 tsp vegetable oil

1 Add all the ingredients except the oil to a food processor with a pinch of salt and blitz until smooth. Transfer the batter to a jug, cover with cling film and leave to rest in the fridge for 1 hr.

2 Heat oven to 220C/200C fan/gas 7. Spoon a tsp of oil into 8 holes of a muffin tin and place in the oven for 5 mins to get really hot. Remove the tin from the oven and carefully pour the batter into the hot oil. Return to the oven and bake for 25–30 mins until risen and deep golden brown. To freeze, cool completely first. Reheat and crisp in a hot oven.

Nutrition per pudding
kcal 140 • fat 4g • saturates 0.4g • carbs 22g • sugars 0.2g • fibre 1g • protein 4g • salt 0.3g

Veggie protein chilli

A protein-packed vegan chilli, perfect after a run or gym workout. This easy supper is simple to make and freezable if you want to batch cook.

EASY ⏱ PREP 15 mins COOK 55 mins ◔ SERVES 1 AFTER TRAINING OR 2 OTHERWISE

- 1 tbsp olive oil
- ½ onion, finely chopped
- ½ red chilli, finely chopped
- 1 garlic clove, finely chopped
- 1 small sweet potato, peeled and cut into chunks
- ½ tsp cumin
- ½ tsp paprika
- ½ tsp cayenne pepper
- ½ tsp cinnamon
- 400g can mixed beans
- 400g can chopped tomatoes
- 1 lime, juiced, to serve
- cauliflower rice, to serve

1 Heat the oil in a large saucepan and add the onion, chilli and garlic and cook without colouring for 1–2 mins. Tip in the sweet potato, spices and some seasoning, then pour in the beans and chopped tomatoes. Fill one of the empty cans with water and add to the pan, then bring to the boil and turn down to a simmer.

2 Cook for 45–50 mins or until the sweet potato is soft and the sauce has reduced – add some water if the sauce looks a bit thick. Stir through the lime juice, season to taste and serve with cauliflower rice. Will freeze for up to 2 months.

Nutrition per serving (1)
kcal 658 • fat 17g • saturates 2g • carbs 88g • sugars 32g • fibre 23g • protein 25g • salt 1.1g

Orange, oat & sultana cookies

These cookies are packed with goodness from wholmeal flour and oats and sweetened with dried fruit and mashed banana.

EASY ⏱ PREP 30 mins COOK 20 mins 🕐 MAKES 16

- 100g butter, at room temperature
- 100g light soft brown sugar
- 50g mashed ripe banana
- 1 tsp vanilla extract
- 1 egg
- ½ tsp grated orange zest
- 100g wholemeal flour
- ¼ tsp salt
- 1 tsp baking powder
- 100g rolled oats
- 25g desiccated coconut
- 50g chopped walnuts
- 75g sultanas or dark chocolate chips

1 Heat oven to 180C/160C fan/gas 4. Cream the butter and sugar together until well blended and smooth. Gradually beat in the banana, vanilla extract and egg. Add the zest. Mix well with a wooden spoon until thoroughly blended.

2 In a large bowl, mix the flour, salt, baking powder, oats, coconut, walnuts and sultanas or chocolate chips. Stir the dry ingredients into the wet and mix thoroughly until a thick dough is formed. Line a baking sheet with parchment. Drop heaped tbsps onto the sheet, leaving a 5cm space around each one, and press down lightly. Bake for 15–20 mins until lightly browned. Cool. Freeze in batches in bags.

Nutrition per cookie
kcal 167 • fat 9g • saturates • 5g • carbs 19g • sugars 11g • fibre 2g • protein 3g • salt 0.18g

Easiest ever biscuits

The simplest biscuits you and the kids will ever bake. We've stamped clean toys into these to decorate them – try your own favourite patterns.

EASY ⏱ PREP 10 mins COOK 10 mins ⏱ MAKES 24

- 200g unsalted butter, softened
- 200g golden caster sugar
- 1 large egg
- ½ tsp vanilla extract
- 400g plain flour, plus extra for dusting

1 Heat oven to 200C/180C fan/gas 6 and line a baking sheet with baking parchment. Put the butter in a bowl and beat it with electric beaters until soft and creamy. Beat in the sugar, then the egg and vanilla, and finally the flour to make a dough. If the dough feels a bit sticky, add a little bit more flour and knead it in. The dough can be frozen at this point.

2 Pull pieces off the dough and roll them out to about the thickness of two £1 coins on a floured surface. The easiest way to do this with small children is to roll the mixture out on a baking mat. Cut out shapes using a 9cm biscuit cutter, or a use the rim of a small glass and peel away the leftover dough around the edges. Press some clean toys gently into the biscuits, making sure you make enough of a mark without going all the way through. Re-roll any off-cuts and repeat.

3 Transfer the whole mat or the individual biscuits to the baking sheet and bake for 8–10 mins or until the edges are just brown. Leave to cool for 5 mins, then serve. Will keep for 3 days in a biscuit tin or freeze in bags in batches.

Nutrition per biscuit
kcal 161 • fat 7g • saturates 4g • carbs 21g • sugars 8g • fibre 1g • protein 2g • salt 0g

Steamed chocolate, stout & prune pudding

A dark and fruity stout brings out the flavour of dark chocolate in Diana Henry's simple steamed pudding. Pour on our decadent chocolate sauce and enjoy.

MORE EFFORT ⏱ PREP 35 mins COOK 1 hr 45 mins plus overnight soaking ⏳ SERVES 10

- 200g prunes
- 175ml stout or a dark, fruity beer (Theakston's Old Peculier is good, or try a fruit beer, particularly one with damsons)
- 175g butter, at room temperature, plus more for the basin
- 30g cocoa powder
- 150g plain flour
- ½ tsp bicarbonate of soda
- 2 tsp baking powder
- 190g soft dark brown sugar
- 3 medium eggs, lightly beaten
- 80g walnuts, 30g blitzed in a food processor, 50g toasted
- 75g dark chocolate (70% cocoa solids), chopped

FOR THE CHOCOLATE SAUCE
- 175g plain chocolate, chopped
- 100ml double cream
- 75ml stout or dark fruity beer
- 175g soft light brown sugar
- crème fraîche or cream, to serve

1 Put the prunes in a dish with the stout and leave to soak overnight. The next day, strain and reserve the stout, and set the prunes aside.

2 Butter a 1.5-litre pudding basin really well. Sift the cocoa powder together with the flour, bicarb and baking powder. Beat the butter and sugar together until fluffy, then gradually add the eggs, a little at a time, beating well after each addition. Fold in the sifted ingredients, alternating with the reserved stout, followed by all the walnuts, the dark chocolate and soaked prunes. Scrape the batter into the prepared basin.

3 Put a piece of baking parchment on top of a sheet of foil (both large enough to cover the top of the basin). Fold a pleat along the middle, then place, parchment-side down, on top of the pudding, with the pleat across the centre. Tie firmly in place with string, using the string to make a handle. Trim the excess parchment and foil.

4 Put the pudding in a large saucepan with a lid, then pour in enough boiling water to come one-third of the way up the side of the basin. Bring the water to a simmer, cover the pan and steam the pudding for 1¾ hrs, making sure that the pan doesn't boil dry. Leave to sit for 10 mins.

5 For the sauce, put the chocolate in a bowl. Pour the cream, stout and sugar into a heavy-bottomed saucepan and heat gently, stirring until the sugar has dissolved and the mixture is hot, then pour over the chocolate. Leave to sit for 2 mins or so. Stir until smooth.

6 To turn the pudding out, run a knife around the edge of the basin. Set a serving plate on top of the pudding, invert, give it a bit of a shake and it should slide out. Pour some of the chocolate sauce over the top and offer the rest in a jug, with some crème fraîche or whipped cream on the side. The whole pudding can be frozen in the basin; defrost thoroughly and reheat in a pan.

Nutrition per serving
kcal 676 • fat 39g • saturates 19g • carbs 69g • sugars 56g • fibre 5g • protein 9g • salt 0.8g

Double choc peanut butter cookies

What could be better with a glass of cold milk than a warm, gooey peanut butter cookie? These choc chunk treats are topped with crunchy chopped peanuts.

EASY ⏱ PREP 20 mins COOK 10 mins ⏲ MAKES 12

- 100g unsalted butter, softened at room temperature
- 100g light brown sugar
- 100g caster sugar
- 1 egg, beaten
- 150g self-raising flour
- 2 tbsp cocoa powder
- ¼ tsp salt
- 200g milk chocolate, 150g chopped into chunks and 50g melted for drizzling
- 75g peanut butter (crunchy or smooth is fine)
- handful of salted peanuts, roughly chopped
- milk to serve (optional)

1 Heat the oven to 180C/160C fan/gas mark 4 and line 2 baking trays with parchment. Using a food mixer or electric whisk, beat the butter and sugar together until light and fluffy. Add in the egg and whisk to combine then beat in the flour, cocoa powder, salt and chocolate chunks until fully incorporated. Using a spoon swirl the peanut butter through the cookie dough.

2 Scoop the dough into 12 large cookies onto the 2 trays using a dessert spoon, leaving plenty of room between each cookie as they'll spread. You can freeze scoops of dough on a tray and then tip them into a bag. Bake in the oven for 9–10 mins until still soft and melty in the middle. They will look underbaked but will harden once cool. Drizzle over the melted milk chocolate and top with a few chopped peanuts and a pinch of flaky sea salt. Serve with a glass of milk for dunking.

Nutrition per cookie
kcal 328 • fat 19g • saturates 9g • carbs 36g • sugars 26g • fibre 2g • protein 6g • salt 0.4g

Passion fruit, chocolate & coconut roulade

This twist on a classic roulade uses the tropical flavours of passion fruit and coconut to create a terrific tropical centrepiece for your table.

MORE EFFORT ⏱ PREP 1 hr COOK 30 mins ◔ SERVES 10-12

- oil or butter, for greasing
- 150g dark chocolate, chopped into small pieces
- 6 large eggs, separated
- 170g golden caster sugar
- 25g cocoa powder
- 25g ground almonds
- 250g tub mascarpone
- 400ml double cream
- 50ml Malibu (optional)
- 85g icing sugar
- 125g passion fruit curd
- 3 ripe passion fruits, flesh scooped out
- 75g coconut flakes, toasted
- edible gold glitter (optional)

1 Heat oven to 180C/160C fan/gas 4. Grease a 33 x 23cm Swiss roll tin and line with greased baking parchment. Tip the chocolate into a heatproof bowl over a pan of gently simmering water. Melt, stirring, then remove and cool.

2 Put the egg whites in a clean bowl, and the yolks and sugar in another. With clean beaters, whisk the whites until they are just soft peaks. Transfer the beaters to the yolks and beat until the sugar dissolves and the mix is thick and pale.

3 Add a large spoonful of whites to the yolks and mix with a metal spoon to loosen the yolks. Add the remaining whites and gently fold in, avoiding knocking out too much air.

4 When nearly all incorporated, sieve the cocoa over the surface, scatter over the almonds and pour in the melted chocolate. Continue folding until the mixture is combined, then scrape into your tin. Spread to the edges and level the surface. Bake for 15–18 mins on the middle shelf of the oven until the surface is crisp and the cake feels springy.

5 While warm, turn the roulade out onto baking parchment, removing the parchment you used for baking. Make a shallow incision about 1cm in from one of the shorter edges, without cutting all the way thorough. Starting from this end, roll up as tightly as you can, bending the cut piece inwards to get the centre of the roll tight. The parchment will help you and stop the layers sticking. Leave to cool.

6 Whisk the mascarpone, cream, Malibu and icing sugar until softly whipped. Carefully unroll the roulade – it will crack in places, but don't worry. Spread a third of the cream all over the surface, leaving a 1.5cm border all the way around. Drizzle the curd over and top with passion fruit.

7 Starting from the end that you used before, re-roll as tightly as you can, bending the cut piece into the cream to get the centre tight. Place seam-side down on a board, spread the cream all over, press in the coconut and dust with glitter. Chill and serve within a few hours. Leftovers will keep for 2 days or freeze whole before putting the cream on.

Nutrition per serving (12)
kcal 545 • fat 41g • saturates 25g • carbs 35g • sugars 34g • fibre 3g • protein 7g • salt 0.2g

Chocolate-orange steamed pudding with chocolate sauce

A classic chocolate-orange flavour in a rich and squidgy dessert, which is low in sugar but no less tasty!

MORE EFFORT ⏱ PREP 25 mins COOK 1 hr 30 mins 🕒 SERVES 8

FOR THE CHOCOLATE SAUCE
- 50g cocoa
- 50g butter, plus extra for greasing
- 100g Total Sweet (xylitol)
- 1 tsp vanilla extract
- 200ml semi-skimmed milk

FOR THE PUDDING
- 1 small orange
- 100g Total Sweet (xylitol)
- 225g self-raising flour
- 50g cocoa
- 150ml semi-skimmed milk
- 1 tsp vanilla extract
- 2 large eggs

1 First, make the sauce. Sift the cocoa into a small saucepan, add all the other ingredients, then warm over a medium-high heat, stirring. Allow to bubble hard for 1 min to make a glossy sauce. Spoon 4 tbsp into the base of a lightly buttered, traditional 1.2 litre pudding basin. Leave the rest to cool, stirring occasionally.

2 Put a very large pan (deep enough to enclose the whole pudding basin) of water on to boil with a small upturned plate placed in the base of the pan to support the basin.

3 Zest the orange, then cut the peel and pith away, and cut between the membrane to release the segments. Put all the pudding ingredients, except the orange segments, in a food processor and blitz until smooth. Add the orange segments and pulse to chop them into the pudding mixture. Spoon the mixture into the pudding basin, smoothing to the edges.

4 Tear off a sheet of foil and a sheet of baking parchment, both about 30cm long. Butter the baking parchment and use to cover the foil. Fold a 3cm pleat in the middle of the sheets, then place over the pudding, buttered baking parchment-side down. Tie with string under the lip of the basin, making a handle as you go. Trim the excess parchment and foil to about 5cm, then tuck the foil around the parchment to seal. Lower the basin into the pan of water, checking that the water comes two-thirds of the way up the sides of the basin, then cover the pan with a lid to trap the steam and simmer for 1½ hours.

5 Carefully unwrap the pudding – it should now be risen and firm – and turn out of the basin on to a plate. The pudding can be cooled and frozen at this point. Spoon over some warmed sauce and serve the rest separately with slices of the pudding.

Nutrition per serving
kcal 338 • fat 10g • saturates 6g • carbs 50g • sugars 4g • fibre 3g • protein 9g • salt 0.5g

Nutty baklava

Our version of this syrup-soaked pastry is gently spiced with cinnamon and cardamom, and has a blend of pecans, pistachios and walnuts.

MORE EFFORT ⏱ PREP 40 mins COOK 1 hr 5 mins 🕑 MAKES 24–28 PIECES

- 200g butter, plus extra for greasing
- 200g pistachios
- 50g walnuts
- 50g pecans
- 3 tbsp honey
- 2 x 270g packs filo pastry

FOR THE SYRUP
- 250g golden caster sugar
- 50g honey
- 2 tsp orange blossom water
- ½ tsp ground cinnamon
- ¼ tsp ground cardamom (from 3 pods)

1 Heat oven to 180C/160C fan/gas 4 and grease a 21cm x 21cm square cake tin with butter. Chop the nuts into small pieces using a food processor, taking care not to blitz them to a paste. Put them into a bowl, stir in the honey and a pinch of salt and set aside.

2 Melt the butter in a pan over a low heat. Cut the first pack of filo pastry sheets in half (so that they fit the tin). Put one sheet in the tin and brush with the melted butter. Lay another sheet on top and brush with butter again. Keep layering like this until the whole pack is used up.

3 Spread the honey and nut mixture over the pastry and press it down lightly with the back of a spoon. Open the other pack of filo, cut in half and continue the layering and buttering process. When you reach the last sheet, pour any remaining butter over the top to finish. Use a sharp knife to cut deep lines into the pastry to create either squares or diamond shapes then bake in the oven for 20 mins.

4 Reduce the heat to 150C/130C fan/gas 2 and bake for a further 45 mins. While the baklava cooks put all the syrup ingredients into a saucepan and add 200ml water. Heat gently until the sugar has dissolved, then boil the mixture for 8–10 mins or until it has reduced to the consistency of runny honey.

5 When the baklava comes out of the oven, pour the warm syrup over the top, allowing it to run into the lines you have cut. Leave it to soak in and serve when it's completely cold. To freeze wrap in cling film, or cut into portions and freeze in batches.

Nutrition per serving (28)
kcal 224 • fat 12g • saturates 4g • carbs 24g • sugars 13g • fibre 2g • protein 4g • salt 0.3g

Peanut butter parfait with salted caramel crunch

Serve this delicious salted caramel, peanut butter dessert chilled, or frozen as a cheat's ice cream.

EASY ⏱ PREP 10 mins plus chilling NO COOK ⏲ SERVES 2

- 100ml double cream
- few drops of vanilla extract
- 75g smooth peanut butter
- 50g icing sugar
- 20g banana chips, crushed, plus 6 whole to serve
- 2 tbsp salted caramel sauce
- 50g peanut brittle, crushed

1 Whisk the cream with the vanilla until just starting to stiffen. In a separate bowl, beat the peanut butter with the icing sugar to slacken, then fold the peanut butter mixture and the crushed banana chips into the cream. Tip into a container. Chill in the fridge for a few hours or overnight, or freeze.

2 To serve, paint a stripe of salted caramel sauce over 2 large plates, then scatter the stripe with the crushed brittle.

3 Using a dessert spoon, scoop the parfait into an oval shape (a quenelle) and sit it on one side of the plate. Top the parfait with a standing row of 3 banana chips, then serve.

Nutrition per serving
kcal 862 • fat 59g • saturates 29g • carbs 67g • sugars 61g • fibre 4g • protein 13g • salt 0.8g

Maple, banana & pecan pop pies

Serve up these sweet and nutty mini fruit pies with a drizzle of colourful icing and thick double cream or custard.

EASY ⏱ PREP 55 mins plus chilling COOK 20 mins ⏲ MAKES 6

- 1 tsp cornflour
- 3 tbsp light brown soft sugar
- 5 tbsp maple syrup
- ½ tsp ground cinnamon, plus a pinch
- 2 bananas, chopped in small pieces
- 320g sweet shortcrust pastry sheet
- 1 egg, beaten
- 100g icing sugar
- 50g pecans, finely chopped
- cream or custard, to serve (optional)

1 In a small bowl mix the cornflour, sugar, 2 tbsp maple syrup and cinnamon to make a thick paste; season with a pinch of salt. Toss the chopped banana through the mixture. Unroll the pastry sheet and use a pizza wheel to cut in half lengthways down the centre.

2 Cut each half into 3 equal rectangles so that you have 6 rectangles in total. Turn a piece of pastry so the long side is nearest to you and fold it in half like a book, to create a fold down the middle. Open the pastry out and spoon the fruit filling onto one side, leaving a border of about 1cm around the edge. Brush the beaten egg around the edges and fold the pastry again to encase the filling. Use a fork to seal the edges all the way around, then brush all over with more egg. Poke a few air holes in the top with the fork. Repeat with the remaining pastry and filling. Arrange the pop pies on a baking sheet lined with baking parchment and chill for at least 30 mins, or for up to 24 hrs. Alternatively freeze for up to 2 months.

3 Heat oven to 200C/180C fan/gas 6. Bake the pop pies for 20 mins, or until the pastry is golden and the filling is bubbling through the holes. Remove from the oven and cool for at least 20 mins. If cooking from frozen, bake for an extra 5 mins. Meanwhile mix the remaining maple syrup with the icing sugar and a pinch of cinnamon and salt to make a thick icing. Spread thinly over the pies and sprinkle with pecans. Eat warm, or cold, for breakfast or drizzle with cream or custard for dessert.

Nutrition per serving
kcal 486 • fat 21g • saturates 6g • carbs 67g • sugars 46g • fibre 2g • protein 5g • salt 0.5g

Frozen blackberry yogurt

Showcase ripe, seasonal blackberries in this simple-to-make dessert with honey and Greek yogurt.

EASY ⏱ PREP 5 mins plus 30 mins standing, plus freezing NO COOK 🕐 SERVES 4

- 200g blackberries
- 40g golden caster sugar
- 300g Greek yogurt
- 50ml honey
- 100ml goat's milk

1 Toss together the blackberries and golden caster sugar in a large bowl. Leave for 30 mins or until the fruit starts to break down, then mash the berries a little with a fork.
2 In a separate bowl, mix the Greek yogurt with the honey and goat's milk. Spoon the yogurt mixture into a freezable container, then tip the berries on top and swirl them through. Freeze for 2 hrs, then give a little stir and return to the freezer to firm up. Take out of the freezer a few mins before serving to soften for scooping.

Nutrition per serving
kcal 208 • fat 9g • saturates 6g • carbs 26g • sugars 26g • fibre 2g • protein 5g • salt 0.2g

Cheat's pineapple, Thai basil & ginger sorbet

An easy blended sorbet with vibrant Thai basil and spicy ginger. Try serving with a drizzle of vodka or white rum.

EASY ⏱ PREP 5 mins plus overnight chilling NO COOK ◕ SERVES 6

- 1 large pineapple, peeled, cored and cut into chunks
- juice and zest 1 lime
- 1 small piece of ginger, sliced
- handful Thai basil leaves, plus a few extra little ones to serve
- 75g white caster sugar
- vodka or white rum (optional)

1 A couple of days before eating, tip everything into a blender or smoothie maker with 200ml water and blitz until very smooth. Pour into a freezable container and freeze overnight until solid.

2 A few hours before serving, remove from the freezer and allow to defrost slightly so it slides out of the container in a block. Chop the block into ice cube-sized chunks and blitz in the blender or smoothie maker again until you have a thick, slushy purée. Tip back into the container and refreeze for 1 hr or until it can be scooped out.

3 To serve, scoop the sorbet into chilled bowls or glasses and top with extra basil. If you want you can drizzle with something a little more potent, such as vodka or white rum.

Nutrition per serving
kcal 145 • fat 0g • saturates 0g • carbs 33g • sugars 33g • fibre 3g • protein 1g • salt 0g

Dark chocolate, banana & rye loaf

We've adapted swimmer Jazmin Carlin's favourite muffin recipe into a loaf that's free from unrefined sugars, flours and dairy. A great snack for on the go.

EASY 🕐 PREP 15 mins COOK 55 mins ⏲ SERVES 8–10

- 50ml extra virgin olive oil, plus extra for greasing
- 150g rye flour
- 100g spelt flour
- 2 tsp baking powder
- 50g cocoa powder
- 2 large eggs, beaten
- 200ml coconut milk
- 80ml maple syrup
- 3 ripe bananas, mashed
- 50g dark chocolate, roughly chopped

1 Heat oven to 180C/160C fan/gas 4. Grease and line a 900g loaf tin. In a large bowl, combine all the dry ingredients except the chocolate. In a separate bowl, whisk together the oil, eggs, coconut milk and maple syrup, then stir in the bananas. Pour the wet ingredients onto the dry and stir to combine. Add the chocolate, then spoon into the prepared tin.

2 Bake in the centre of the oven for 50–55 mins until a skewer inserted into the middle of the loaf comes out clean. Leave to cool in the tin, then remove and cut into slices to serve. Will keep in an airtight container for 3–4 days, or freeze for up to 3 months – warm in the oven before serving.

Nutrition per serving (10)
kcal 273 • fat 13g • saturates 6g • carbs 31g • sugars 12g • fibre 4g • protein 6g • salt 0.3g

Strawberry & cinnamon streusel bars

Pack these in tins for picnics or school fetes, or serve single bars with a dollop of clotted cream for dessert. Blackberries also work really well when strawberry season is over.

MORE EFFORT ⏱ PREP 10 mins COOK 55 mins ◔ MAKES 12

- 300g hulled strawberries
- juice and zest ½ lemon
- 300g plain flour
- 175g golden caster sugar, plus 3 tbsp for the topping
- 1½ tsp ground cinnamon
- 1 vanilla pod, halved lengthways
- 250g pack butter, 200g at room temperature, 50g cold and diced
- 4 tbsp rolled porridge oats
- 3 tbsp chopped hazelnuts
- 2 tbsp strawberry jam

1 Heat oven to 180C/160C fan/gas 4 and line a 22cm square tin with baking parchment. Slice the strawberries thinly and mix well with 4 tsp lemon juice, then put them in a sieve over a bowl and set aside to macerate, discarding the liquid that drips into the bowl.

2 Put the flour, 175g caster sugar, 1 tsp cinnamon and ½ tsp salt in a food processor. Scrape in the seeds from the vanilla pod, then add the softened butter and pulse until the mixture comes together. Spoon out a quarter of the mixture into a mixing bowl and set aside. Tip the rest of the mixture into the bottom of your tin and press down firmly to make an even base. Prick a few times with a fork, then bake for 25 mins until golden.

3 While the base is cooking, add the cold butter, remaining sugar, the oats, hazelnuts, remaining cinnamon and the lemon zest to the reserved mixture. Use your fingers to rub together until crumbly.

4 When the base is done, mix the sliced strawberries with the jam and arrange on top. Sprinkle over the crumbly topping and bake for another 30–35 mins until the top is golden and the strawberries juicy and bubbling. Leave to cool completely in the tin before cutting into bars or squares. Will freeze tightly wrapped in cling film.

Nutrition per bar
kcal 381 • fat 20g • saturates 11g • carbs 44g • sugars 23g • fibre 2g • protein 4g • salt 0.5g

Chocolate hazelnut ice cream cheesecake

No one will guess that this easy, rich and creamy no-cook, make-ahead cheesecake uses only 4 ingredients – ideal for a dinner party.

EASY ⏱ PREP 15 mins plus overnight freezing NO COOK ⏱ SERVES 12

- 200g honey nut cornflakes
- 2 x 400g jars chocolate hazelnut spread
- 2 x 180g tubs full-fat cream cheese
- 1 tbsp roasted and chopped hazelnuts

1 Put the cornflakes and half a jar of chocolate hazelnut spread in a bowl and beat to combine – don't worry about breaking up the cornflakes. Press the mix into the base of a 23cm springform tin.

2 In a separate bowl, beat the cream cheese until smooth, then fold in the remaining chocolate hazelnut spread. Smooth onto the cornflake base, wrap tightly in cling film and freeze overnight.

3 Remove from the freezer 30 mins before serving, or until you can cut it easily with a sharp knife. Serve in slices with hazelnuts sprinkled over. Will keep in the freezer for up to 1 month.

Nutrition per serving
kcal 542 • fat 33g • saturates 15g • carbs 50g • sugars 42g • fibre 3g • protein 8g • salt 0.5g

Tropical granola lollies

Simple fruity lollies that count as one of your 5-a-day, topped with rich dark chocolate and crunchy cereal for a moreish frozen treat.

EASY ⏱ PREP 10 mins plus overnight freezing COOK 10 mins ◔ MAKES 8 X 75ML LOLLIES

- 2 large mangoes, peeled, destoned and roughly chopped
- 2 large ripe bananas, peeled and roughly chopped
- 8 tbsp coconut milk
- 100g granola
- 100g dark chocolate

1 Purée the mango, banana and coconut milk in a blender until rich and smooth. Pour the mixture into lolly moulds and freeze overnight.

2 The next day, whizz the granola slightly in a small food processor to remove any large lumps (or tip into a bowl and bash with the end of a rolling pin), then tip into a bowl.

3 Melt the chocolate in a heatproof bowl set over a pan of simmering water, making sure the base of the bowl isn't in contact with the water.

4 Remove the lollies from their moulds. Dip the tops one at a time in the chocolate, then into the granola. Place on a tray lined with baking parchment to set – they will set very quickly. Eat immediately or freeze until needed.

Nutrition per serving
kcal 223 • fat 9g • saturates 5g • carbs 30g • sugars 22g • fibre 4g • protein 3g • salt 0g

Gooey toffee puddings

Indulgent yet wonderfully light, these individual caramel sponges are baked with a sticky toffee sauce – keep in the freezer for a last-minute pud.

EASY ○ PREP 30 mins plus cooling COOK 30 mins ○ MAKES 8

- 140g softened butter, plus extra for greasing
- 200g light muscovado sugar
- 3 large eggs, beaten
- 175g self-raising flour
- cream or ice cream, to serve (optional)

FOR THE SAUCE
- 75g light muscovado sugar
- 75g dark muscovado sugar
- 75g butter
- 150ml double cream

1 Lightly grease 8 mini metal pudding basins that each hold around 200ml. Place a small disc of baking parchment in the base of each one.
2 To make the sauce, put the sugars and butter in a small saucepan and cook over a low heat until the butter melts and the sauce is glossy, stirring regularly. Add the cream and bring to a simmer. Cook for 1 min, stirring constantly. Remove from the heat and divide among the pudding basins. Leave to cool for 30 mins.
3 Heat oven to 200C/180C fan/gas 6. Beat the butter, sugar, eggs and flour together in a large bowl with a wooden spoon or electric whisk until pale and thick. Spoon the mixture into the pudding basins and place them in a small roasting tin.
4 Add cold water to the roasting tin until it rises just 1cm up the sides of the basins. Place the tin in the oven and bake for about 25 mins or until well risen and a skewer inserted comes out clean.
5 Take the tin out of the oven and, one at a time and holding firmly with a dry tea towel, loosen the sides of each pudding with a round-bladed knife. Turn out onto 8 warmed dessert plates, or arrange on a platter. Serve hot with cream or ice cream, if you like. Cool completely and wrap tightly in clingfilm if you want to freeze them.

Nutrition per pudding
kcal 572 • fat 34g • saturates 21g • carbs 60g • sugars 44g • fibre 1g • protein 5g • salt 0.7g

Index